Horse Trails of "Colorful" Colorado

Northern Colorado – Book 1

(Contains trails from Larimer, Weld and Yuma Counties)

**201 Trails with Pictures & Information of Importance
To
Horseback Riders**

By

Janet M. St. Jacques

Horse Trails of "Colorful" Colorado

Northern Colorado– Book 1

Published by: Ride The Western Trails Publications
2204 Eagle Drive, Loveland, Co 80537

First Edition

ISBN 0-9763431-0-X

TX 6-113-641

A good man is concerned for the welfare of his animals

Proverbs 12:10

The Lord says, "I will guide you along the best pathway for your life. I will advise you and watch over you."
Psalm 32:8

Table of Contents

Foreword

Over the years, my friends and I have traveled many miles with our horses. Finding trails to ride fitting our needs tended to be both challenging and frustrating. Sometimes we heard about trails from other horse owners. Many trails were found by driving around in our vehicles, stopping to explore potential candidates. As the years passed by, more and more information became available on the internet but details about the trails were lacking or non-existent. Much of the information that was found was geared toward hikers or bicyclists. Searching the internet was time consuming and often confusing. If the trail hadn't been checked out prior to the ride, disappointment was always a possibility. Many times we found that parking for our horse trailer(s) was impossible or the trail was more advanced than we felt comfortable riding our horses on. We searched for books finding many on hiking, biking and jeep trails but very few, if any, could be found on horse trails. These are the reasons I was motivated to write this first book in a series on Horse Trails of "Colorful" Colorado. I wanted to give horse owners one reference that had a description of the trail, a map and pictures as well as other important information. I hope you enjoy reading and especially riding the trails that are in this book as much as I have had in putting it together.

Disclaimer

Horseback riding can be dangerous even when riding a well trained horse with an experienced rider. Information contained within these pages has been gathered from many sources. At publication, every effort was made to ensure the accuracy of the information. Even though a GPS unit was used, like cell phones, satellite coverage was at times intermittent. This information is published for general reference and not as a substitute for independent verification by users when circumstances warrant. The author, Janet St. Jacques, sponsors, advertisers and/or anyone contributing information to this book will not be held responsible for any inconvenience or injury resulting from the use or misuse of the maps, diagrams or text contained within this book.

Definition of "Difficulty" Rating

EASY: These trails are great for the beginning trail rider or inexperienced horse. Elevation is gradual and minimal. The trail has no obstacles and footing is good.

MODERATE: These trails are for the rider or horse that has completed several trail rides. There are more obstacles (easy-to-cross bridges, slow moving, shallow water crossing, etc.) and/or steeper climbs. The footing may have a few rocky spots and/or narrow paths.

DIFFICULT: These trails are strenuous for both the rider and the horse. There are many obstacles (bridges may be narrow and high above the ground, water may be fast moving and deep, etc.) and/or very steep climbs. The footing may be very rocky and there may be portions of the trail where you need to get off your horse and walk. The trail itself may be very long. These trails need an experienced rider and a well conditioned, well trained, experienced trail horse. If you are "curling your toes" in your boots, you know that you are on a difficult section of the trail.

Trail Etiquette

- Park in such a way as not to block anyone else in.
- Be considerate if space is limited and park so others will have room to park.
- Say "hello" to the people you meet on the trails. We need to share trails and spreading good will among other trail users can help avoid potential conflict.
- Bicyclers yield to hikers and horses. Hikers yield to horses.

- Downhill trail users must "always" yield to uphill trail users.
- Stay on the trails to avoid and not disturb wildlife. If you need to move off the trail, ride within 10 feet of the trail. You may ride beyond the 10 feet limit briefly to avoid imminent danger to other persons.
- Approach turns in anticipation of someone around the bend.
- Be prepared for the unexpected by being aware of what is going on around you. A horse does not take time to reason, they react by instinct.
- If your horse is a kicker, put a red ribbon on its tail as a warning. Remember, you are responsible for controlling your horse on the trail.
- When you need to pass someone on the trail, call out "passing on your left" to warn them.

Trail Etiquette

(Continued)

- If you are being passed, pull off to the right and try to have your horse face the trail. Do not turn the horse so that they have to pass his/her rear end and risk being kicked.
- Remember the gate rule – if a gate is open, leave it open – if a gate is closed, close it after you ride through.
- Carry out all trash. Try to leave your camp and trails even cleaner than when you found them.
- Don't ride and drink alcohol. You need your best judgment to ride and handle your horse through trail obstacles.
- Do not clean out your horse trailer of manure and/or wood shavings at the parking lot. Even though manure is totally bio-degradable, keep the parking area as clean as possible by moving and scattering any manure off to the grassy area. Don't leave the impression to other trail users that horses "litter."
- During hunting season, wear plenty of hunter orange on yourself as well as on your horse.

Arapahoe & Roosevelt National Forests Regulations Regarding Horses

- Horses are prohibited overnight in the following areas:
  - Comanche Peak Wilderness travel zones
    - Browns Lake
    - Comanche Lake
    - Emmaline Lake
    - North Fork
  - All named developed campgrounds (except for **Jack's Gulch Campground** on the Pingree Park road

- Certified **Weed-Free Hay or Cubes** "must" be used in the National Forest.

- Do not tie animals to live trees.

- When stopped, keep animals at least 200 feet from lakes, streams and trails.

- In Wilderness Areas, remember the "12 Heartbeat Rule." There should be no more than 12 heartbeats in a group. Horse, dog and human each count as one heartbeat. Groups exceeding 12 are to separate and maintain at least a 1 mile distance while riding or camping.

- Unless otherwise posted, horses are allowed when camping on forestland including designated **dispersed** campsites.

- No camping at trailheads.

General Location Map

(This map is for reference only; the map is NOT to scale)

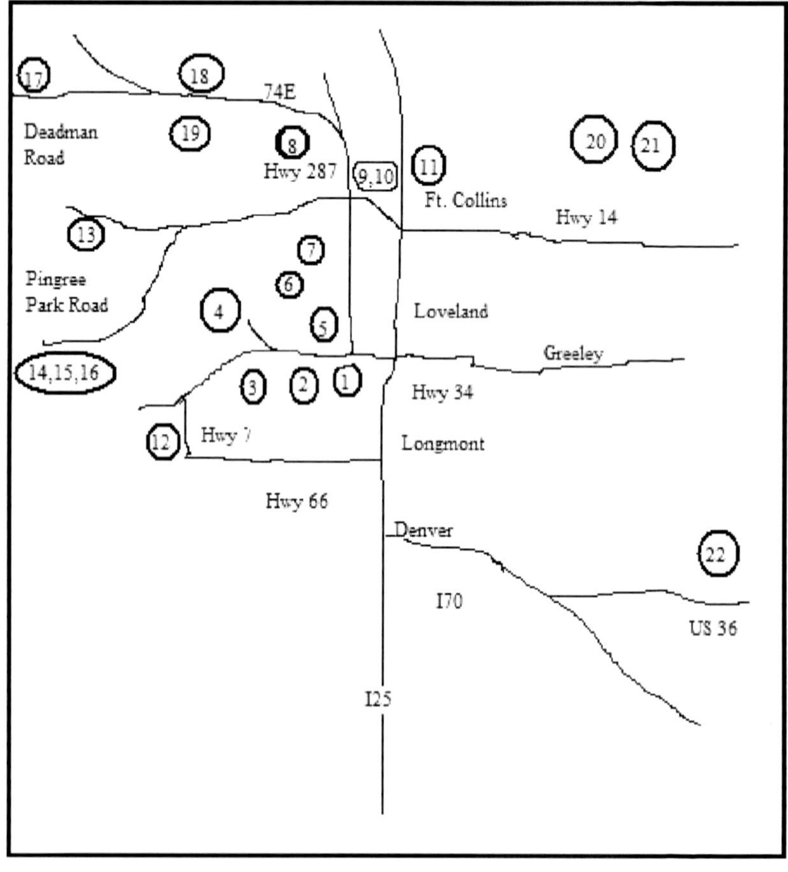

Trail # 1

Trail Name:

Ramsay-Shockey Open Space, Pinewood Res. (Larimer)

Govt. Organization: Larimer County Parks and Open Lands

Fees: You "must" get your daily park permit or receive a fine of $50. As of this writing, $6 daily or yearly pass of $65 resident, $75 non-resident. The annual pass is currently valid at Horsetooth Reservoir, Horsetooth Mountain Park, Carter Lake, Pinewood Reservoir, FlatIron Reservoir and Ramsay-Shockey Open space.

Beginning Elevation: 5,765 ft.

Ending Elevation: 6,580 ft.

Trailer Parking: Parking can be limited based upon usage. No designated spots for horse trailers

Facilities: At the trailhead, restrooms and domestic drinking water are available

Difficulty: Easy

Length of Trail: Approximately 7 miles round trip

Trail Usage: Horseback riding, hiking, mountain biking
Dogs are permitted on leash.

Directions: From I-25 travel west on US 34 (Loveland exit) approximately 11.3 miles. Turn south (left) on 29S and continue for 2 miles. Turn west (right) on 18E. At approximately 2 miles, turn left (look for sign) to obtain park permit from The Bison Visitor Center or Self-Service Station across from the visitor center. After purchasing pass, get back on 18E and continue for approximately 6 miles to the first parking area (4 miles will be steep with curves). First parking area is Blue Mountain. If parking is not available, continue past the 2nd parking lot (Launch Area) and continue on to the 3rd parking area (Ramsay-Shockey)

Sign showing turn for buying park pass

Bison Visitor Center

Self-Service Station across from visitor center

1st parking lot (Blue Mountain)

2nd parking lot, boat Launch Area, do "not" park here

3rd parking lot, Ramsay-Schockey

Do "not" ride across the dam

If parking at Ramsay-Shockey, ride your horse toward Dead End. Road turns to dirt, with trailhead on the left at the bottom of hill

Trailhead if parked at Ramsay-Shockey parking lot

Restrooms at the trailhead

Part of the Shoshone Trail

One of the many bridges along the trail

View of Pinewood Reservoir from trail

Do "not" cross bridge, use trail to the right

Trail passes through small meadow

View from Besant Point Trail

Besant Point Trail, dismount and walk your horse

Coming up to the Blue Mountain parking lot

Picnic area at Blue Mountain parking lot

General Information: The Ramsay-Shockey Open Space is adjacent to Pinewood Reservoir. Camping sites are available but accommodations are not available for overnight camping with horses. Parking can become limited, especially during the weekends. If you park at the Ramsay-Shockey parking lot, you will need to ride your horse from the parking area, north, down the Dead End road to the trailhead for Shoshone Trail. Do not ride your horse over the dam trail. The Shoshone Trail is dirt trail with a gradual climb away from the reservoir, "head to tail," that winds through areas of trees as well as small meadows. On a clear day, the views are spectacular. Along the trail there are a few bridges that span marshy areas that are easy to cross. There is one bridge that you and your horse will take an alternate path around. At a point on the Shoshone Trail loop, you will have the option to head south and ride the Besant Point Trail to the Blue Mountain Trailhead. If you choose this route, the trail follows the Pinewood Reservoir shoreline. This trail is very easy but it is out in the open with no shade. As you get close to the Blue Mountain Trailhead, you will encounter a bridge that is wheelchair accessible. Dismount and walk your horse; this bridge can be slippery. Continue to the Blue Mountain Trailhead where there are picnic tables and restrooms. To get back to the Ramsay-Shockey parking lot, retrace your route on the Besant Point Trail until you reach the point where it intersects the Shoshone Trail loop. Here you have the option to retrace your previous route on the Shoshone Trail by turning left or to continue straight around the reservoir to eventually end at the trailhead at the Dead End road. This could be considered a perfect trail for a "first" ride of the season. From what I have observed, this area is mostly used by fishermen and campers. I have seen very few people hiking on these trails. I have never seen bikers, but I have seen bike tracks.

Notes:

Map:

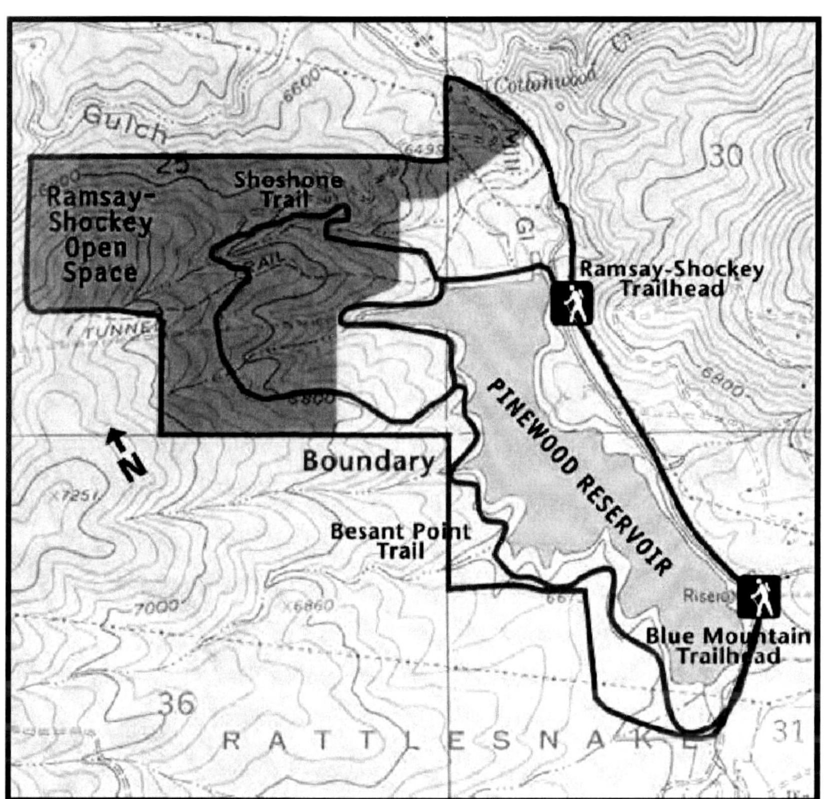

National Geographic Map #101

Trail #2
Trail Name:

Summit Adventure Trail, Round Mountain (Larimer)

Govt. Organization: Larimer County Parks and Open Lands & Arapaho-Roosevelt National Forest

Fees: None

Beginning Elevation: 5,785 ft.

Ending Elevation: 8,535 ft.

Trailer Parking: Parking easily accommodates large trailers with ample room to navigate.

Facilities: At the trailhead, restrooms are available. This is a "dry" trail, no water is available.

Difficulty: Moderate to Difficult. Portions of trail are extremely rocky, narrow and steep

Length of Trail: Approximately 9.5 miles round trip

Trail Usage: Horseback riding, hiking, mountain biking
Dogs are permitted on a leash.

Directions: From I-25 travel west on US 34 (Loveland exit) approximately 16.8 miles. The trailhead is on the south (left), across the highway from Loveland's Viestenz-Smith Mountain Park.

Parking area

Restroom facilities

Trail begins on other side of gate

Take the left trail at fork

First .3 mile with a gradual climb

Follow signs, trail will start to get rough & narrow

The 1st mile is rocky, narrow and hugs the side of the mountain

Narrow path through rock field that hugs side of the mountain

This is a fair representation of the majority of the first mile

After the 1st mile, the trail starts to move away from the side of the mountain and gets less rocky

As the trail winds more to the interior of the mountain, the trail becomes easier

Information is posted along the trail about various subjects

View of Big Thompson Canyon about 1 mile into trail

General Information: The initial stretch of this trail is a deceptively simple path. The Summit Adventure Trail and the Foothills Nature Trail start off together for a short distance and then the Summit Adventure Trail takes off to the left. The trail does a gradual climb, following roads that are used by the city of Loveland for water and power maintenance. Where the road ends, the trail starts on the left and embarks on a steep two mile climb straight up the side of the Big Thompson Canyon. The trail is extremely narrow and rocky, hugging the side of the mountain. Approximately .5 miles in, you will need to travel a trail that is chiseled through a rock field. Unless you have a very sure footed horse and nerves of steel, I would walk my horse the first mile. After you reach the 1 mile marker, the trail starts to wind its way slowly toward the interior of the mountain. Mileage signs beside the trail mark each mile you complete. Interpretive signs, explaining the landscape and plant life, are also found along the way. It's a steady climb, using switch backs, to the summit. The trail will level out for a bit in some spots. The trail is shady and the surrounding view is beautiful. The last .5 miles is another steep climb to the summit. This is a trail for a well conditioned and sure footed horse. This is not a trail for an inexperienced trail rider.

Notes:

MAP: **Use for Summit Adventure Trail & Foothills Nature Trail**

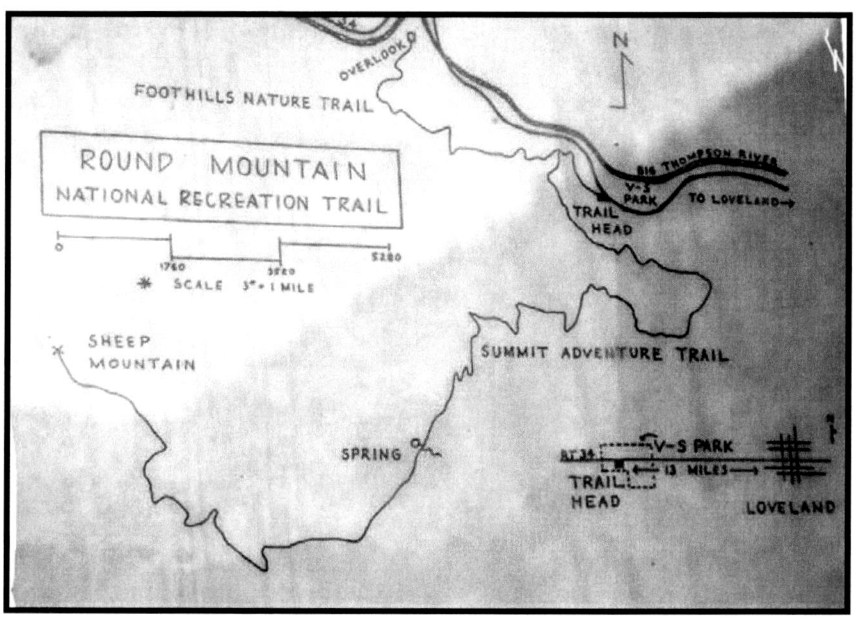

National Geographic Map #101

Trail #3
Trail Name:

Foothills Nature Trail, Round Mountain (Larimer)

Govt. Organization: Larimer County Parks and Open Lands & Arapaho-Roosevelt National Forest

Fees: None

Beginning Elevation: 5,785 ft.

Ending Elevation: 6,245 ft.

Trailer Parking: Parking easily accommodates large trailers with ample room to navigate.

Facilities: At the trailhead, restrooms are available. This is a "dry" trail, no water is available.

Difficulty: Easy

Length of Trail: Approximately 2 miles round trip

Trail Usage: Horseback riding, hiking, mountain biking
Dogs are permitted on a leash.

Directions: From I-25 travel west on US 34 (Loveland exit) approximately 16.8 miles. The trailhead is on the south (left), across the highway from Loveland's Viestenz-Smith Mountain Park.

**See pages 22, 23 (Summit Trail) for pictures of parking and trailhead

**See page 30 (Summit Trail) for map

Continue straight on the trail

Trail is a wide service road with pine trees on both sides

Water pipe line along trail

Beware of Bears!

Rocks outlining a drainage area

Path becomes narrow & forks off to the right

Trail becomes a little rocky from here to the top

At the top of the trail, a stone hut

View of Thompson Canyon & Hwy. 34 from trail

From the stone hut, take the trail to the south for a different route down to the service road

General Information: This trail uses the same trailhead as the Summit Adventure trail and is the only characteristic that they have in common. Unlike the Summit Adventure trail, the Nature Trail climbs slowly in elevation and is very wide with only one slightly rocky section. Trees line both sides of the trail, giving a nice shady ride on a hot day. Glimpses of the Thompson Canyon and Hwy. 34 can be seen from various spots along the trail to the north. At approximately .9 miles into the ride, the trail will fork off to the right. From here, the trail becomes narrow and a little rocky. At the top of the trail is a small stone hut. The views from here are breathtaking. On your return trip, you can either go down the way you came or take the trail that goes off to your right from the stone hut. If you take the trail to your right, it will take you back to the spot where the service road forked. This trail would be great as a first trail ride in the mountains. Be sure to have bells on your horse; bears have been sighted in this area. Also, the trail is very popular with hikers.

Notes:

Trail #4

Trail Name:

North Fork Trail, Dunraven Trailhead (Larimer)

Govt. Organization: Arapaho-Roosevelt National Forest, Comanche Peak Wilderness & Rocky Mountain National Park

Fees: None

Beginning Elevation: 7,776 ft.

Ending Elevation: 10,668 ft.

Trailer Parking: Parking easily accommodates large trailers with ample room to navigate.

Facilities: At the trailhead, restrooms are available. Water is available for your horse from the river along the trail.

Difficulty: Moderate, bridges & water crossings, a little rocky as well as a steady climb

Length of Trail: Approximately 5.5 miles round trip to the "Meadows", approximately 9 miles round trip to Rocky Mountain National Park boundary, approximately 18.4 miles round trip to Lost Lake.

Trail Usage: Horseback riding & hiking. Dogs are permitted on a leash until you reach Rocky Mountain National Park where dogs are "not" allowed.

Directions: From I-25 travel west on US 34 (Loveland exit) approximately 26 miles toward Estes Park to the Drake turn-off. Turn northwest (right) on County Road 43 and travel about 6 miles to Country Road 518 (Dunraven Glade Road). Turn north (right) and travel approximately 2 miles to the trailhead.

Ample parking at trailhead

Restroom at North Fork Trailhead

One of the many bridge/water crossings

Stopping for a drink along the trail

Riding through ¼ mile of private property (Cheley Camp)

Set of 3 easy steps & trail continues to the left

The only water crossing where you can not use the bridge

Stopping to let the horses eat at the Meadows

Just one of the outstanding views along the trail

One of the open areas you will ride through

River was running after spring run-off

Heading back to the trailhead after an awesome ride

Herd of elk along the road to the trailhead

General Information: When you reach the end of Dunraven Glade Road, you will notice two trailheads. They are the Bulwark Ridge Trails (consisting of Indian Trail (1 mile to trailhead), Miller Fork Trail (3 miles to trailhead) and Signal Mt (6 miles to trailhead)) and the North Fork Trail to the left of the Bulwark Ridge Trails. This describes the North Fork Trail only.

The North Fork Trail begins at an elevation of 7,776 feet, drops down into the North Fork drainage through the Comanche Peak Wilderness and steadily climbs to an elevation of 10,700 feet ending at Lost Lake in Rocky Mountain National Park. On this particular day, we rode as far as the border of the Rocky Mountain National Park before turning around to go back to the trailhead. The trail is well marked, reasonably wide, with the majority of the trail ridden "head to tail." Until the trail reached the "Meadows," it follows the North Fork of the Big Thompson River. There are at least 6 water crossings via wooden bridges. All but one crossing (on the far side of Cheley Camp, which is a ¼ mile of private land you need to ride through) will allow horses to cross through the water. Be aware that especially during the spring, this is a rushing, noisy stream. Expect to see horses at Cheley Camp; the stable is right next to the trail. Cheley Camp is a summer and fall camp for kids from 13 to 17 years of age. Prior to the "Meadows," the trail is moderately rocky in places. The "Meadows" is a great place to stop and let your horses rest and eat. If you continue on the trail past the "Meadows," the trail starts to climb steeper and becomes rockier as you approach Rocky Mountain National Park. If you continue on through Rocky Mountain Nation Park, the trail becomes the Lost Lake Trail. Most of the trail travels through spruce and lodgepole pine forest. Riding with bells on your horse would be a good idea; there are numerous blind spots along the trail as well as a bear warning at the trailhead. If your horse is comfortable with water crossings and bridge crossings, this is an excellent ride.

Notes:

MAP:

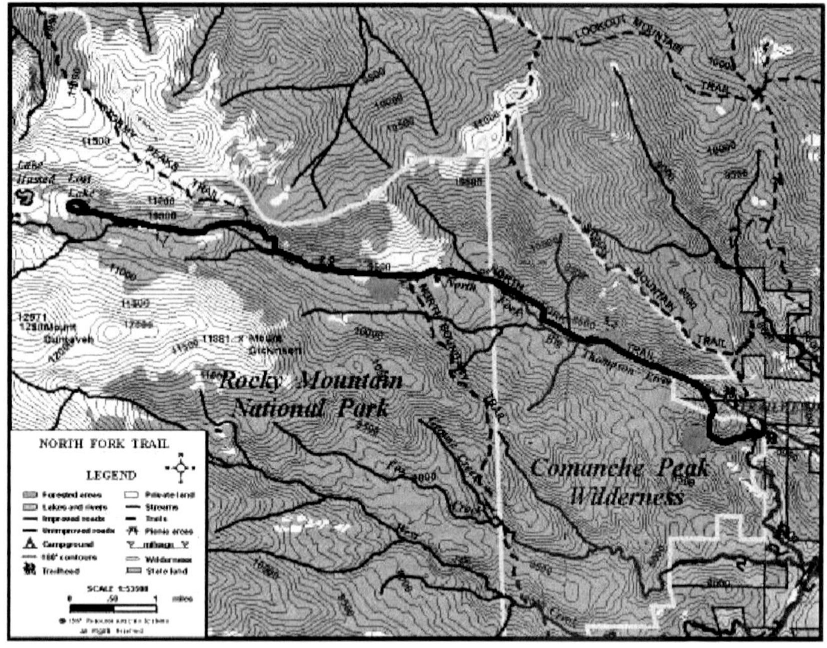

National Geographic Map #101

Trail #5
Trail Name:

Devil's Backbone Trail (Larimer)

Govt. Organization: Larimer County Parks and Open Lands

Fees: None (as of this writing, Larimer County is considering charging the same fee as charged for Horsetooth Mountain Park)

Beginning Elevation: 5,075 ft.

Ending Elevation: 5,475 ft.

Trailer Parking: Parking easily accommodates large trailers with ample room to navigate. There are designated spots just for horse trailers.

Facilities: At the trailhead, restrooms and domestic drinking water is available as well as water for your horse.

Difficulty: Easy to Moderate with one difficult section. This section is on the upper part of the trail where it is very narrow and steep with slippery rocks and no place to get off the trail if someone is approaching in the opposite direction.

Length of Trail: Approximately 7 miles round trip

Trail Usage: Horseback riding, hiking, mountain biking
Dogs are permitted on a leash.

Directions: From I-25 travel west on US 34 (Loveland exit) approximately 8.2 miles to Hidden Valley Drive (you will see a large concrete water tower on your north (right), just west of Hidden Valley Drive). Turn here and proceed north for approximately 1/4 mile. The trailhead is in the northwest part of the parking lot. There is a different trailhead for hikers and bikers.

Entrance

Ample Parking Area

Restroom Facilities

Water

Gate

Rattlesnake Warning

Trail separates, horses ride to the left

Horses take the trail to the right

First 1/3rd of trail is easy

Extremely rocky & narrow, 2/3^{rds} into the trail

Another rock section, 2/3rds into trail

Take the right fork of Wild Trail, trail will loop back

Wild Trail (last 1/3rd), a little rocky and steep

Spectacular views along the trail

Enjoying a ride

Picnic Area at trailhead

General Information: This is one of the most impressive geologic landmarks in Larimer County with beautiful views. The trailhead has been recently improved to accommodate the many varied users of this trail. Note that horses start off from the trailhead along a different path than hikers. Approximately ¼ mile down the trail, there is a small gate just large enough to accommodate 1 horse. The terrain, where the entry gate is located, is on a slight incline. Because the gate is narrow and supported with a spring type hinge, it closes quickly and may hit your horse as you pass through. The trail starts a gradual climb from this spot on. At various points along the way, the path will split designating a separate route for horses. Water is unavailable along the trail, but is available at the parking area. Wear plenty of sunscreen for shade is non-existent. This trail is heavily traveled and can be challenging when meeting hikers, bikes or other horses at the narrow and/or rocky portions of the footpath. Rattlesnakes also make their homes in this terrain. Be cautious and alert and stick to the trail. At the end of your ride, relax and enjoy your lunch at the picnic area. In order to miss the crowds, I would suggest riding during the week.

Notes:

MAP:

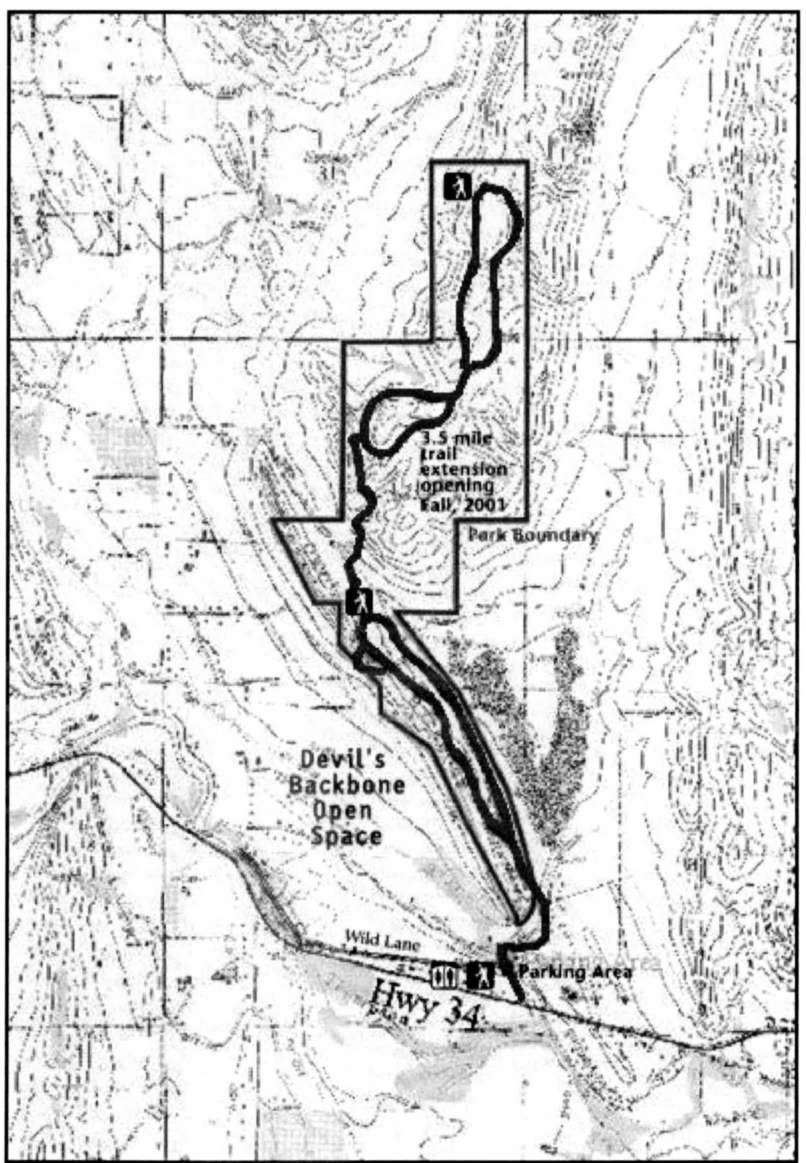
3.5 mile
trail
extension
opening
Fall, 2001
Park Boundary
Devil's
Backbone
Open
Space
Wild Lane
Parking Area
Hwy 34

Trail #6
Trail Name:

Coyote Ridge/Rimrock Open Space (Larimer)

Govt. Organization: City of Ft. Collins and Larimer County

Fees: None

Beginning Elevation: 5,150 ft.

Ending Elevation: 5,600 ft.

Trailer Parking: Parking easily accommodates large trailers with ample room to navigate.

Facilities: Approximately 1 mile into the trail, restrooms are available. Water is "not" available for you or your horse.

Difficulty: Easy to Moderate with two difficult sections involving stairs bordered by landscape timbers.

Length of Trail: Approximately 7 miles round trip (Coyote Ridge 4.5 miles, Rimrock 2.5 mile loop)

Trail Usage: Horseback riding, hiking, mountain biking
Dogs are "not" permitted.

Directions: From I-25 travel west on US 34 approximately 6.5 miles to Wilson. Turn north (right) and proceed north for approximately 5 miles. Turn west (left) into the parking lot for the Coyote Ridge trailhead. The trail is about halfway between Loveland and Ft. Collins, south of the Larimer County Landfill.

Parking Area

Trailhead

The beginning of trail with a reminder to stay within 10 ft. of the trail

First mile has a wide trail with a gradual climb

Restroom, continue on left fork of trail to top of Coyote Ridge

Small "bridge" on the trail to the top of Coyote Ridge

Upper trail is narrow and rocky in places

Keep to the right

Top of Coyote Ridge & beginning of Rimrock Open Space

Stone steps will be found at various spots along the trail

Rough trail ahead, dismounting is advised

Dismount and walk your horse on these steps

Trail continues down to loop through the valley & back up to Coyote Ridge

General Information: After leaving the parking area, there is a small opening that leads you to the trail. For the first mile, the trail is wide with a gradual climb as it is an old road. The trail begins to climb as you approach a small uninhabited cabin, used for presentations. The public restroom is located in this area. For the next mile the trail begins to wind its way around the hogbacks and finally up to the summit of Coyote Ridge. Along this 2.25 mile stretch, there are a few blind spots that are marked that you need to be aware of. On the top of Coyote Ridge, you will have views of the Plains to the East and the majestic Rockies to the west as well as the cities of Loveland and Ft. Collins. If you continue on the trail, you will make the transition from Coyote Ridge to the Rimrock Open Space. As you begin descending into the valley of the Rimrock Open Space, there are stairs bordered by landscape timbers. A sign is posted prior to the stairs asking you to dismount. The stairs are at a steep angle, very narrow and close together and it is best to walk your horse down as well as up on your return trip. From here the trail continues to descend into the valley. The trail will loop around the valley and bring you back to this point. There is one other set of stairs along the loop that we did not dismount. Depending on your comfort level, you may want to dismount and walk your horse down these steps. I found this trail to be a very relaxing, enjoyable ride with beautiful views. Do not be surprised to see deer and coyotes and be aware that snakes make their home in this area.. In order to avoid the crowds, it's best to ride this trail during the week.

Notes:

MAP:

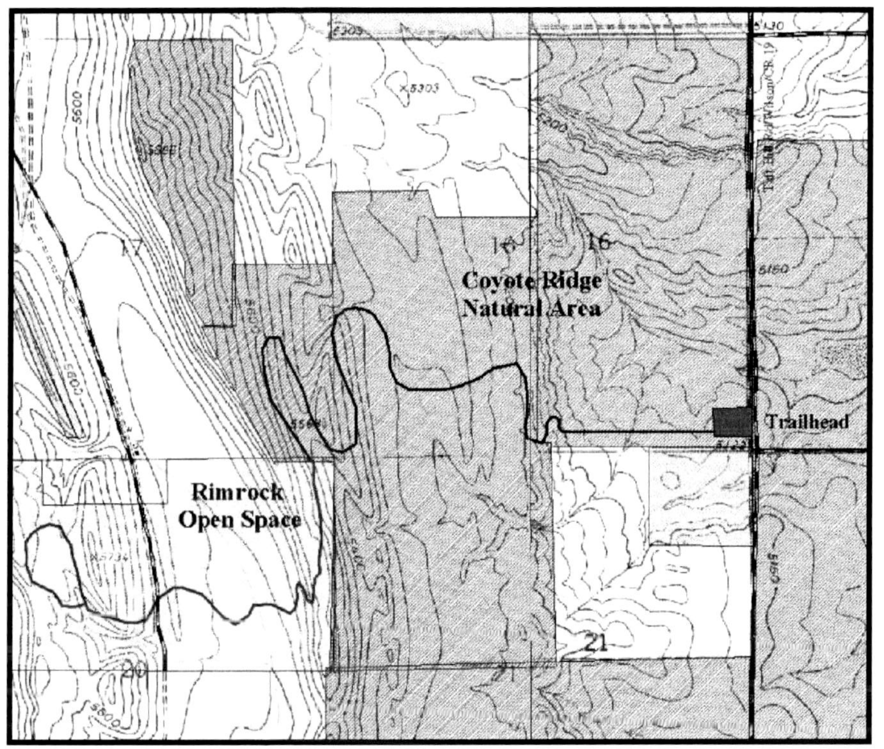
Coyote Ridge
Natural Area
Rimrock
Open Space
Trailhead
17
16
16
20
21
5600
5303
5150

Trail #7
Trail Name:

Horsetooth Mountain Park (Larimer)

Govt. Organization: Larimer County Parks and Open Lands

Fees: You "must" get your daily park permit or receive a fine of $50. As of this writing, $6 daily or yearly pass of $65 resident, $75 non-resident. The annual pass is currently valid at Horsetooth Reservoir, Horsetooth Mountain Park, Carter Lake, Pinewood Reservoir, Flatiron Reservoir and Ramsay-Shockey Open space.

Beginning Elevation: 5,430 ft.

Ending Elevation: 7,255 ft.

Trailer Parking: There are 8 designated spots for horse trailers. If all spots for horse trailers are full, park rangers have stated that you could park on the grassy area by the designated spots.

Facilities: At the trailhead, restrooms are available as well as drinking water, including water for your horses.

Difficulty: Various trails from Easy to Difficult

Length of Trail: See map (page 76) for the various trails and the length

Trail Usage: Horseback riding, hiking, mountain biking
Dogs are permitted on a leash.

Directions: From I-25 travel west on US 34 approximately 10.8 miles to County Road 27. Turn north (right) toward Masonville and continue 9.4 miles to stop sign. Turn east (right) on County Road 38E for approximately 12.7 miles. This road will be slightly winding and will increase in elevation. The trailhead will be on the north (left) side of the road..

Entry to parking area

Horse trailer parking at trailhead

Purchase "Daily Park Permit" here

Restrooms

Picnic area and water for your horse

Trails are clearly marked

Service Road is used frequently for horseback riding

View from along the Service Road trail

Horsetooth Rock Trail can get rocky the nearer you get to Horsetooth Rock

Horsetooth Rock

General Information: Horsetooth Mountain Park is a 2,772 acre park and open space with 28 miles of trails for hiking, mountain biking and horseback riding. During our time at the park, we used the Soderberg Trail, Service Road and part of the Horsetooth Rock Trail. According to the rangers that we talked to at the park, all trails are open to horses but they would not recommend Horsetooth Falls (lots of steps, unsuitable for horses) and Mill Creek Trail (very steep and large boulders). The following is a list of the trails and their classification according to the park rangers:

Easy Trails
Soderberg
Horsetooth Falls
Carey Springs
Nomad

Difficult Trails
Mill Creek

Moderate Trails
Spring Creek
West Ridge
Wathen
Herrington
Stout
Sawmill
Logger's
Horsetooth Rock
Audra Culver

Because the trails link together, it would be to your advantage to take a map with you. Except for the Service Road, the majority of the trails may be rocky, from moderate to extreme. Rattlesnakes are a common site, so be aware and stay on the trail. Mountain lions have also been spotted, especially during a dry season. I would suggest having bells on your horse, to warn animals as well as people, that you are on the trail. On the service road, expect to encounter fast moving bikes coming downhill. This park is heavily used on the weekends, so it would be best to plan a ride during the week. Take a lunch with you; they have a great picnic area at the trailhead.

Notes:

MAP:

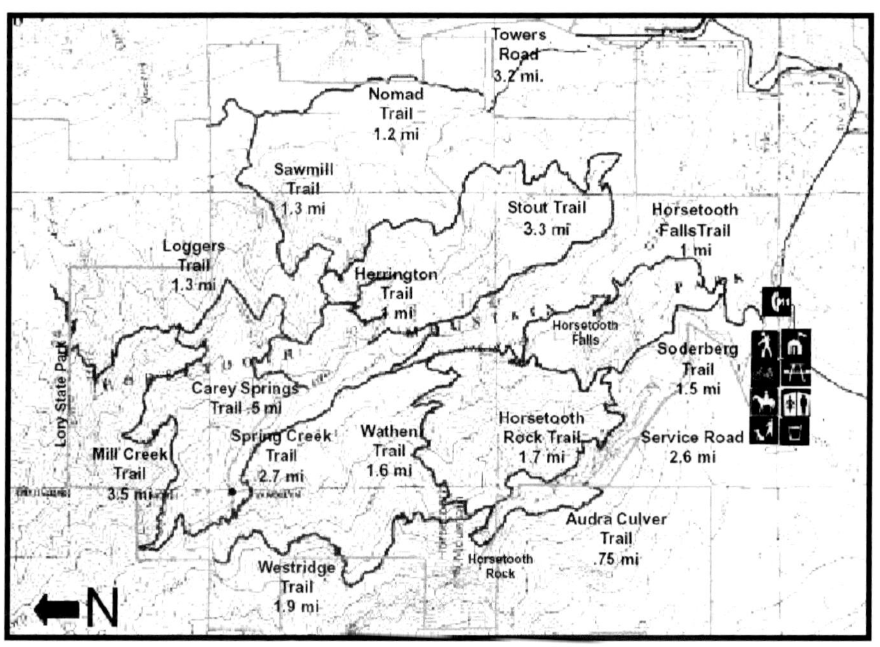
Towers Road 3.2 mi.
Nomad Trail 1.2 mi
Sawmill Trail 1.3 mi
Stout Trail 3.3 mi
Horsetooth Falls Trail 1 mi
Loggers Trail 1.3 mi
Herrington Trail 1 mi
Horsetooth Falls
Soderberg Trail 1.5 mi
Lory State Park
Carey Springs Trail .5 mi
Spring Creek Trail 2.7 mi
Wathen Trail 1.6 mi
Horsetooth Rock Trail 1.7 mi
Service Road 2.6 mi
Mill Creek Trail 3.5 mi
Audra Culver Trail .75 mi
Horsetooth Rock
Westridge Trail 1.9 mi
N

Trail #8

Trail Name:

Lory State Park Trails (Larimer)

Govt. Organization: Colorado State Parks

Fees: You "must" get your DAILY PASS of $5 at the visitor center. An ANNUAL PASS can be bought that is valid at any state park for the remainder of the calendar year. Call (970) 493-1623 for additional information

Beginning Elevation: 5,485 ft.

Ending Elevation: 5,610 ft.

Trailer Parking: Trailers can be parked at the Stables, Eltuck Picnic Area and at the far south parking area.

Facilities: At various trailheads, restrooms are available.

Difficulty: Easy with various bridges to cross

Length of Trail: See Map on page 85 for the various trails and the length

Trail Usage: Horseback riding, hiking, mountain biking
Dogs are permitted on a leash.

Directions: Take U.S. 287 northwest from Ft. Collins through LaPorte, then turn west (left) at the Bellvue Exit, County Road 52E (Vern's Cafe). Proceed approximately 2 miles to County Road 23N. Turn south (left) for 1.4 miles and turn west (right) on County Road 25G. Drive another 1.6 miles to the park entrance.

Park entrance off of County Road 25G

Purchase tickets here at the Visitor Center

Parking area at Eltuck Picnic Area

Restrooms are located at various parking areas

Approaching East Valley Trail

Trails are well marked

Trails are single file, in and out of foliage

One of the many bridges to cross (7 – 8 bridges of various lengths)

South Valley Trail Loop allows an easy transition into Horsetooth Mountain Park

Stopping along trail for a quick bite

View from West Valley Trail looking north

Another small bridge to cross

General Information: Formerly ranch land, the 2,400 acres offer a unique view of rock outcroppings, sandstone hogbacks, grassy open meadows, shrubby hillsides, ponderosa pine forests and Horsetooth Reservoir. Located just inside the park entrance is a newly built Visitor Center. The Visitor Center serves as an entrance station for purchasing park passes as well as an environmental education center. There is ample parking available for your trailer, if you wish to enter the Visitor Center to look around or speak with the rangers. Drinking water is not available on the trails and may be obtained at the Visitor Center. Be sure to pick up a trail map when you purchase your daily pass; not all trails are available for horseback riding.

For our ride, we parked at the Eltuck Picnic Area. From the parking lot, a short trail connected us with the East Valley Trail. The East Valley Trail takes you to the south end parking area where you have the choice of the Shoreline Trail or the South Valley Trail Loop. The Shoreline Trail is a 1 mile ride that leads down to the edge of Horsetooth Reservoir. We rode the South Valley Trail Loop. This trail loops around a cross-country jumping course. At the furthest point of the loop, the trail offers an easy transition into Horsetooth Mountain Park onto the Nomad Trail. Heading back north on the South Valley Trail Loop, you can pick up another trail into the upper elevations of Horsetooth Mountain Park by way of the Mill Creek Trail. Because of time constraints, we did not ride into Horsetooth Mountain Park. Continuing on South Valley Trail Loop, the trail intersects with the West Valley Trail. Here you have the choice of riding the West Valley Trail or going back on the East Valley Trail. We found this ride to be extremely enjoyable. The trail is very well marked with numerous small wooden bridges to cross. It's a narrow trail, so you will be riding "head to tail." The terrain has a gentle grade making for a very relaxing ride. This seems to be a well liked area for hiking and mountain biking. We rode on a Thursday afternoon and saw 4 other horse trailers. Weekends can get busy, so I would suggest calling ahead to see if any special activities are scheduled.

Notes:

Map:

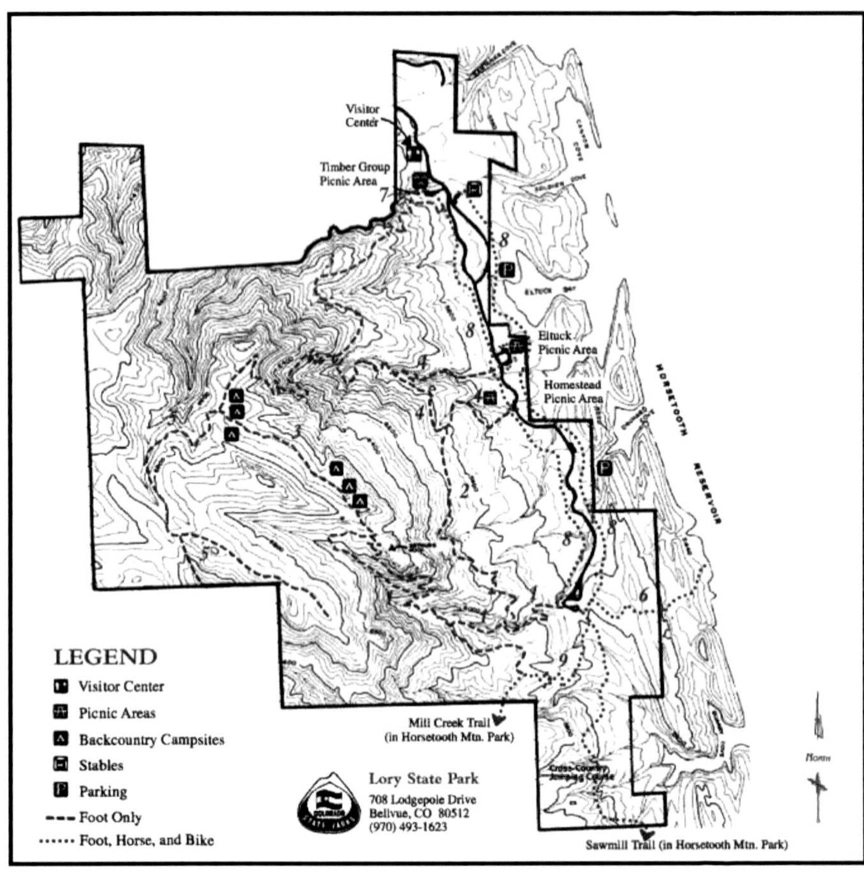

All trail distances are one way

6 Shoreline Trail (Easy) – This comfortable 1 mile ride leads down to the edge of Horsetooth Reservoir.

8 East & West Valley Trails (Easy) – These trails run parallel to the main road, branching to coves at Horsetooth Reservoir or meeting with the mountain trails. East Valley 2.2 miles West Valley 2.3 miles

9 Mill Creek Link (Difficult) – From the south valley trail, this .9 miles link offers passage to the upper elevations of Horsetooth Mountain Park by way of the Mill Creek Trail.

10 South Valley Trail Loop (Easy) – This easy 2.7 mile loop trail takes you to the south border of Lory State Park. This link offers an easy transition into Horesetooth Mountain Park.

Trail #9
Trail Name:

Pineridge Open Space (Larimer)

Govt. Organization: City of Ft. Collins

Fees: None

Beginning Elevation: 5,150 ft.

Ending Elevation: 5,305 ft.

Trailer Parking: Parking easily accommodates large trailers with ample room to navigate if you don't park too close to the Dog Park. There are no designated spots just for horse trailers.

Facilities: A portable restroom potty at Dog Park

Difficulty: Easy

Length of Trail: Approximately 5.8 miles round trip

Trail Usage: Horseback riding, hiking, mountain biking
Dogs are permitted on a leash.

Directions: From I-25 travel west on US 34 (Loveland exit) approximately 6.5 miles to Wilson. Turn north (right) on Wilson and travel approximately 8.9 miles to Horsetooth road (you will pass the trailhead for Coyote Ridge/Rimrock Open Space as well as the Larimer County Landfill). In Ft. Collins, Wilson turns into Taft Hill Road. Turn west (left) on Horsetooth and travel to a dead end at the trailhead.

Parking Area

Parking area is west of barrier

View from parking lot west toward trailhead

Restroom Facilities at Southwest Dog Park

One of the many small bridges

Northwest view from top of ridge

View of Dixon Reservoir

Looking toward Horsetooth Dam from top of ridge

After an enjoyable ride

General Information: From where you parked your horse trailer, you will need to travel a very short distance on Horsetooth Road to the entrance of the trail. Keep in mind that this is also the entrance for the Southwest Dog Park and you may encounter numerous dogs on leash with their owners. (There is another entrance on County Road 42C. As you start to climb the first hill on 42C, you will see the Pineridge parking lot on your left. I found it hard to get in and out of with a trailer because of the hill. The parking area can also get very crowded). The trails are well marked and are in excellent shape. The trails going up to and along the ridge are fairly wide, allowing you to ride "side-by-side." Scattered among the narrow trails are small wooden bridges. The terrain is a mixture of flat areas, steep foothills, slopes and valleys. The peaks of Rocky Mountain National Park as well as Horsetooth Dam can be seen from the top of the west ridge. Habitat includes open water (Dixon Reservoir), mature cottonwood forest, short grass prairie, foothills shrub lands and large areas of Ponderosa Pines. Wildlife includes a large prairie dog colony, deer, mountain lion, rattlesnakes, hawks, eagles, ospreys, pelicans, variety of songbirds, lizards, rabbits, foxes and coyotes. Watch your step; there are prairie dog holes close to the trails, as well as water fowl in the bushes by the reservoir that may surprise you and your horse. These trails can be heavily used by bikers, hikers and joggers, so it's best to plan your ride during the week days.

Notes:

MAP:

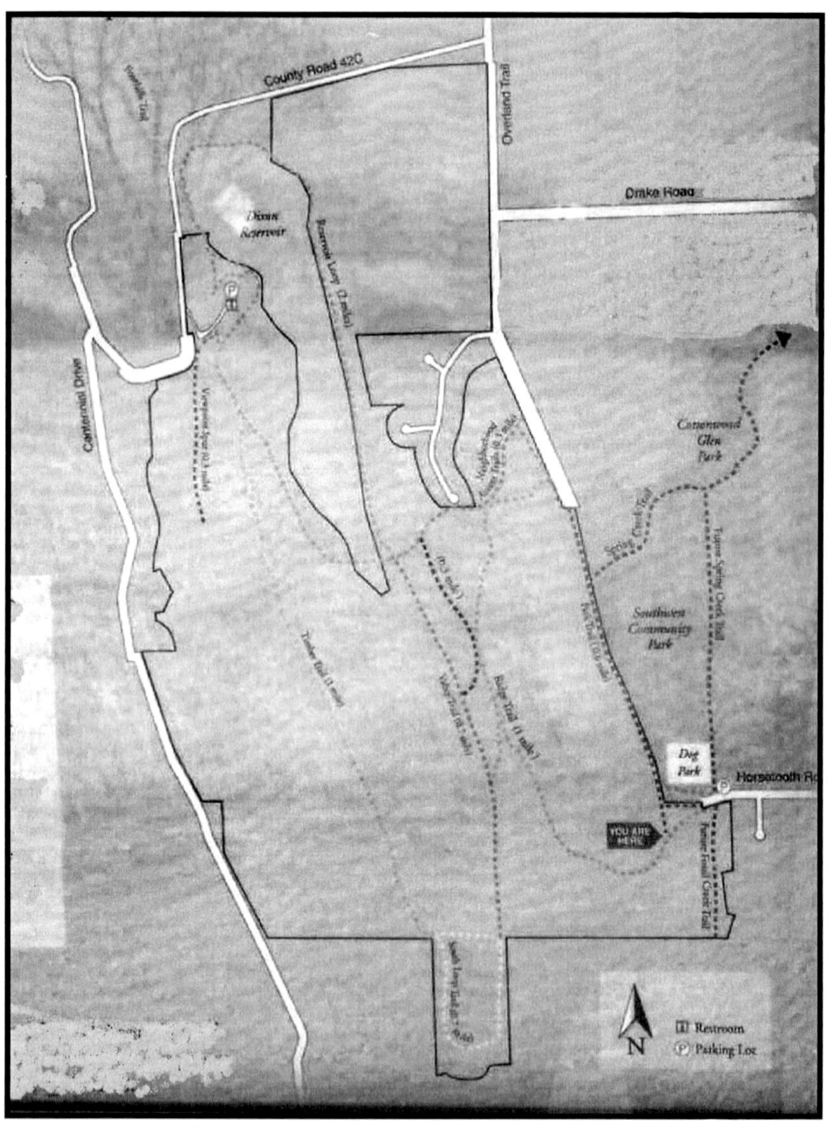
County Road 42C
Overland Trail
Drake Road
Centennial Drive
Dixon Reservoir
Cottonwood Glen Park
Southwest Community Park
Dog Park
YOU ARE HERE
N
Restroom
Parking Lot

Trail #10
Trail Name:

Poudre River Trail (Larimer)

Govt. Organization: City of Ft. Collins

Fees: None

Beginning Elevation: 5,428 ft.

Ending Elevation: 5,428 ft.

Trailer Parking: Parking easily accommodates large trailers with ample room to navigate.

Facilities: Restrooms are not available at trailhead, but can be found at McMurry Natural Area. Water from the Poudre River is available for your horse.

Difficulty: Easy to Moderate due to various underpasses and exposure to in-town noises and high assortment of users of the trail.

Length of Trail: Approximately 16.8 miles round trip

Trail Usage: Horseback riding, walking, biking, jogging, rollerblading Dogs are permitted on a leash.

Directions: From I-25 travel west on US 34 (Loveland exit) approximately 6.5 miles to Wilson. Turn north (right) and proceed north for approximately 13.6 miles. You will pass Coyote Ridge as well as the Larimer County Landfill. Once in Ft. Collins, Wilson turns into Taft Hill Road. Continue north, as you cross Laporte Ave., you will be approximately 1.2 miles from the trailhead. As you go down a small hill, horse stables will be on the right-hand side with the trailhead a short distance beyond them. Be careful, it is easy to miss the turn off.

Ample Parking Area

A group of riders at the start of the trail

First Tunnel Heading south on the Trail

A lot of the trail follows close to the river, away from bike path

Path goes under the road (Shields)

Cross bridge to McMurray Natural Area

Trail travels along the Poudre River

Another obstacle prior to College Ave.

General Information: The Poudre Trail meanders along the Poudre River for 8.35 miles one way. It currently runs between the trailhead at N. Taft Hill Road and the Environmental Learning Center on E. Drake. We started our ride from the trailhead at N. Taft Hill Road and rode to where the trail was currently closed for construction at College Ave. I have been told that you can ride the 8.35 miles to the end, but there is at least one major road that you need to cross in traffic. This trail will expose your horse to many various city noises and situations. You will meet bikers, walkers, skateboarders, rollerbladers and wheelchairs along the trail. The trail is concrete with narrow dirt paths on either side for horses. At various parts of the trail, the dirt path will take off into the trees, away from the concrete trail. Numerous Natural Areas are located along the trail that can be accessed via bridges or off shoot trails. During our ride, we crossed the bridge to the McMurry Natural Area and rode around the various ponds located there. Tunnels are used to go under the majority of the streets that the trail crosses. Expect to hear loud noises from the cars and trucks using the road above you. We dismounted and walked our horses through the tunnels because of the low height and noises. Prior to walking through the tunnels, we also shouted that horses were coming through. We did this because it was hard to tell if someone was coming from the opposite direction. Along the trail you will pass horses in pastures, houses and various businesses. Every time that I have been on this trail, I have seen people riding horses. This trail can be very busy on weekends and during week-days lunch hours. If your horse has never been exposed to a lot of stimuli, I would suggest riding with a friend who may have a horse that has been exposed to these types of conditions or is known to be calm in stressful situations. This would not be a trail for a "green" horse.

Notes:

MAP:

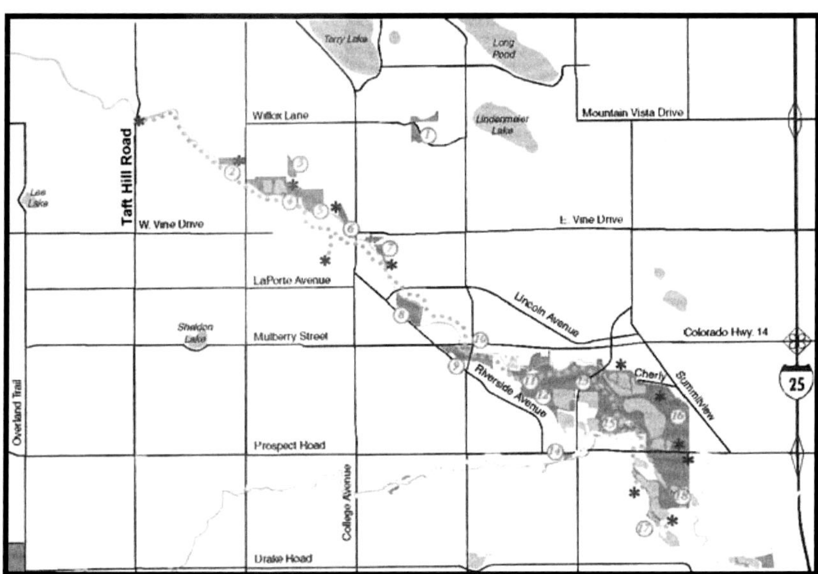

* **Parking Lot**
2 - North Shields Pond Natural Area
3 - Magpie Meander Natural Area
4 - McMurry Natural Area
5 - Salyer Natural Area
7 - Gustav Swanson Natural Area
8 - Udall Natural Area (not yet open to public)
9 - Springer Natural Area
10 - Williams Natural Area
11 - Bignall Natural Area
12 - Nix Natural Area
13 - Kingfisher Point Natural Area
14 - Coterie Natural Area
15 - Cattail Chorus Natural Area
16 - Riverbend Ponds Natural Area
17 - Prospect Ponds Natural Area
18 - Cottonwood Hollow Natural Area

Trail #11
Trail Name:

Arapaho Bend Natural Area (Larimer)

Govt. Organization: City of Ft. Collins

Fees: None

Beginning Elevation: 4,858 ft.

Ending Elevation: 4,858 ft.

Trailer Parking: Parking easily accommodates large trailers with ample room to navigate at the Harmony Transportation Transfer Center. At the corner of Horsetooth Road and Strauss Cabin Road (Larimer County Road 7) is a parking area as well as along Strauss Cabin Road (Larimer County Road 7). Large trailers could be parked at these two areas depending on the vehicles currently parked there.

Facilities: A portable restroom potty is available at the trailhead along Strauss Cabin Road (Larimer County Road 7)

Difficulty: Easy

Length of Trail: Approximately 4.0 miles round trip (250 acres)

Trail Usage: Horseback riding, hiking, mountain biking, fishing
Dogs are permitted on a leash.

Directions: From I-25, exit west on Harmony Road. The Harmony Transportation Center is approximately .01 miles, on the north side. The turnoff for Strauss Cabin Road (Larimer County Road 7) is approximately an additional .2 miles west. Turn north and continue for another .4 miles. The trailhead at Horsetooth and Strauss Cabin Road (Larimer County Road 7), is located approximately .7 miles north of the turn off at Harmony and Strauss Cabin Road.

Parking at the corner of Horsetooth and Strauss Cabin Road (Larimer County Road 7)

Parking along Strauss Cabin Road (Larimer County Road 7)

Parking at rear of Harmony Transportation Transfer Center

Two of the many ponds that the trail surrounds

The majority of the trail is wide, allowing riding "side-by-side"

Beware of water fowl that could spook your horse

General Information: This naturalized gravel mining site has several ponds which provide habitat for bass, yellow perch, and pumpkinseed fish. Cormorants, raccoons, beavers, rabbits, snapping turtles, and skunks also live here. The terrain is mostly flat and the majority of the trail is wide enough to ride "side-by-side." The trail itself is sandy with small stones, making it perfect for riding unshod horses. The trail meanders around the various ponds as well as along the Poudre River. Be prepared to have geese and ducks take flight as you ride by. You can hear the traffic noise from I-25 as you ride on the east trails. You can also hear the traffic from Harmony Road as you ride along the south end of Arapaho Bend. There are spots along the trail where you can ride down the bank into the Poudre River to get your horse accustomed to crossing a river. The ponds are used for fishing and you may come across small non-motorized boats. This could be the perfect site for your first ride after a long winter season. It's also a good ride for a horse that is just starting to be ridden on trails. I have ridden here during the week as well as the weekend and have never found it to be crowded. This is definitely a hidden treasure in Ft. Collins.

Notes:

MAP:

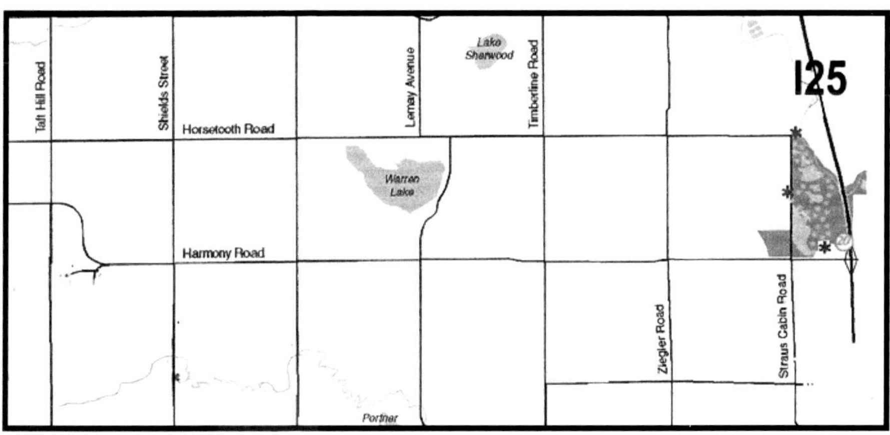

*** - Available Parking**

Trail #12
Trail Name:

Lion Gulch (Larimer)

Govt. Organization: Arapaho-Roosevelt National Forest

Fees: None

Beginning Elevation: 7,325 ft.

Ending Elevation: 8,424 ft.

Trailer Parking: Large parking lot, parking may be limited due to high usage. No designated spots for horse trailers.

Facilities: At the trailhead, restrooms are available. Domestic drinking water is not available. Water from streams/river is available for your horse.

Difficulty: Easy to Moderate (Bridges and small streams)

Length of Trail: 6.2 miles round trip to Homestead Meadows

Trail Usage: Horseback riding, hiking, mountain biking. Dogs are permitted on a leash.

Directions: From I-25 travel west on Hwy. 66 past Hygiene toward Lyons. In Lyons take Hwy. 36 northeast toward Estes Park for approximately 12 miles. There is no landmark or sign that can be seen prior to the trailhead on the left-hand side of the road.

OR

Take Hwy 36 southeast from Estes Park for about 8 miles to the trailhead. There is a blue sign for the Pinewood Fire District just before you get to the trailhead. The trailhead is on the right-hand side of the road.

Be careful, if you pass the trailhead from either direction, finding a place to turn around will be difficult.

Parking area

Restroom facilities

Trailhead

Start of trail

First of the 3 bridges, after crossing take path to the right

Horses take the right fork in trail

You will encounter various "sets of steps" along the trail

Trail does get rocky in spots

One of the 7 stream crossings along the trail

This bridge your horse "must" cross

After a heavy rain, part of the trail became a stream

Many sections of the trail are wide and rock free

As you get close to the Homestead Meadows, the trail widens

Mileage to the various homesteads

One of the Homesteads

Continuing on to additional homesteads will add up to 4 miles one way

A view of the meadows

Heading toward the closest homestead

Small waterfall along trail

Trail meanders through open area

General Information: This was my first trail ride with my horse almost 15 years ago and it is still one of my favorites. The majority of the trail is fairly wide and well maintained. As you leave the trailhead, it immediately starts to descend. The first obstacle you will encounter is the first of 3 wooden bridges. Forging the streams instead of crossing the bridge is possible at two of the bridges. At one bridge (see pictures), the bridge has to be crossed. At one point in the trail, near the beginning, horses need to follow a path away from the hiking trail. The two trails come together again approximately .5 miles later. After crossing the first bridge, the trail is a steady climb and winds its way between the shade of ponderosa pines and open grassy areas. The small stream will be your constant companion. Check out the various waterfalls on your right, approximately 1 mile into the trail. Along the way, you will cross the stream approximately 7 times as well as encounter various fairly rocky areas and "steps" (see pictures). As you get closer to the meadows, the trail widens and allows you to ride "side-by-side." At the meadows, signs are posted pointing to the various homesteads and the appropriate mileage to each. Here you can turn around and go back or continue to one of the further homesteads. The furthest homestead (Pierson Trail) is an additional 4 miles one way.

This is a well known trail for both horseback riding and hikers. I would suggest getting to the trailhead early in the day. Be prepared to meet families with children and dogs on this trail during the week as well as on the weekends.

Notes:

MAP:

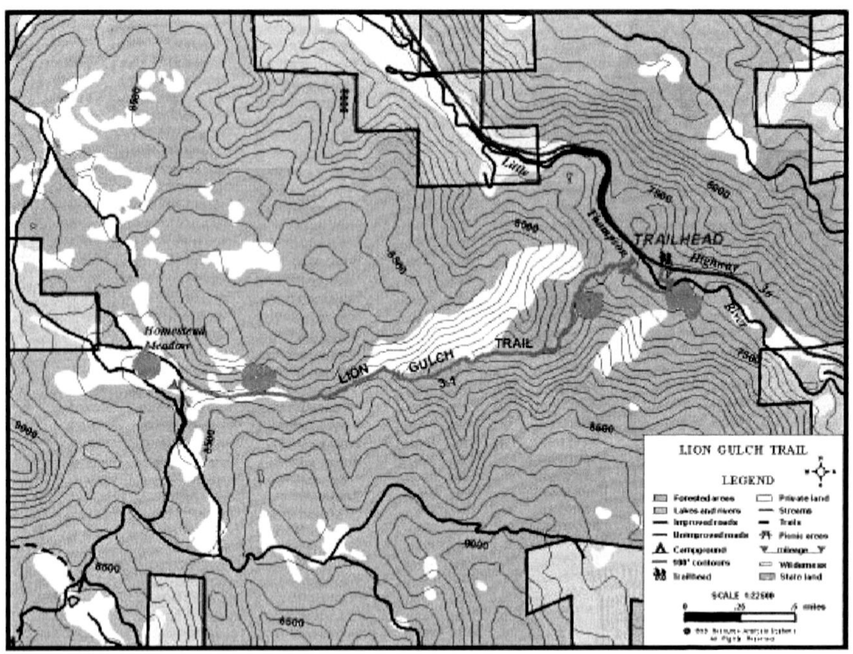

National Geographic Map #101

Trail #13
Trail Name:

Dadd Gulch Trail (Larimer)

Govt. Organization: Arapaho-Roosevelt National Forest

Fees: None

Beginning Elevation: 7,027 ft.

Ending Elevation: 8,456 ft.

Trailer Parking: Parking easily accommodates large trailers with ample room to navigate. Trailers can also be parked in the field behind the fence in the southwest corner of the parking area.

Facilities: The restrooms are located on the north side of Highway 14 across the road from the actual trailhead.

Difficulty: Easy to Moderate. Your horse needs to be in moderate shape and be comfortable in crossing narrow and shallow streams.

Length of Trail: Approximately 7 miles round trip

Trail Usage: Horseback riding, hiking, mountain biking
Dogs are permitted on a leash.

Directions: Go north out of Ft. Collins on Hwy. 287. Turn west (left) at the Poudre Canyon turnoff (Ted's Place). From Ted's Place drive approximately 27 miles up the canyon. The trail will be on your left about ¾ miles west of mile marker 94.

Parking Area

Trailers can be parked in field behind gate

Gated entry to trail

Old corral and loading chute at trailhead

One of the many small meadows along the trail

There's a running stream under this ice

On top, the trail passes along the edge of a clear-cut, offering views of the canyon below.

General Information: This trail is well defined and easy to follow. It is actually the old Dadd Gulch Stock Drive. The trail follows a stream in the bottom of the gulch for about two thirds of its length. Over 15 stream crossings must be made but the stream is narrow and shallow, posing no problems. In the early spring, the trail tends to be boggy in places. Sections of the trail are wide enough for riding "side-by-side," but most of the time it will be "head-to-tail." The trail gently climbs from 7,027 to 8,456 feet in altitude. Most of the trail is easy to ride. A section where the trail climbs out of the gulch is steeper and therefore of more moderate difficulty. The gulch is heavily wooded with juniper, ponderosa pine, aspen, and douglas fir. The trail is somewhat rocky in spots, so shoes for your horse are recommended. At various points along the trail, the remnants of fires can be seen on both sides and the smell of smoke is in the air. I assume that this was a "controlled" burn because of the locations and articles I have read on the internet in regards to clearing this trail of overgrowth. There are also several grassy meadows along the way and adequate water for your horse. Be aware that since this trail is located along the Poudre River, it may be heavily traveled on weekends. A day on this trail makes for a very pleasant ride.

Notes:

MAP:

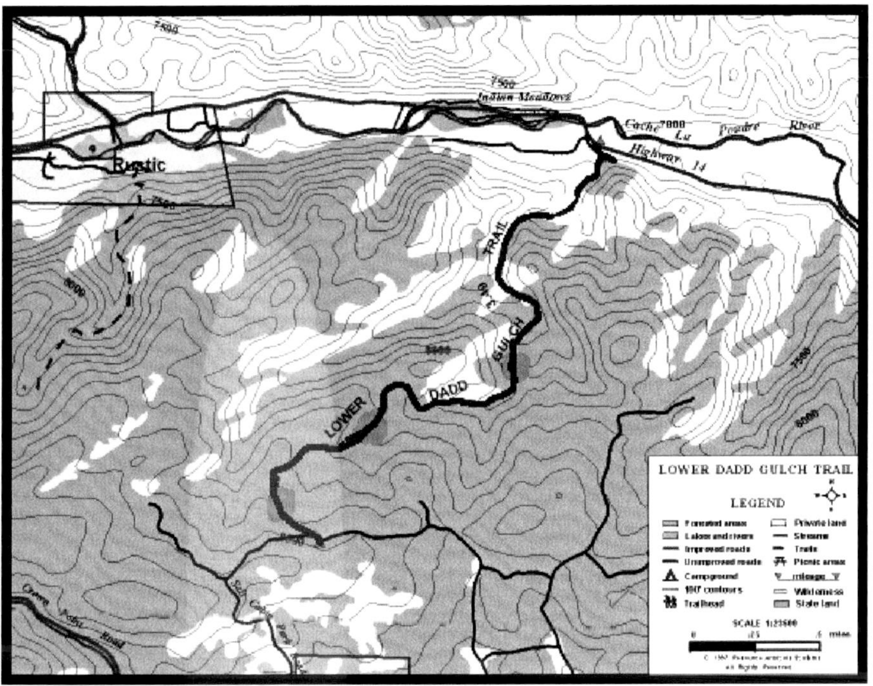

National Geographic Map #112

Trail #14
Trail Name:

Jacks Gulch Campground and Trail (Larimer)

Govt. Organization: Arapaho-Roosevelt National Forest

Fees: Yes, call for fees and opening/closing dates (970-498-2770)

Beginning Elevation: 8,100 ft.

Ending Elevation: 8,100 ft.

Trailer Parking: Ample parking for trailers up to 50 feet

Facilities: Six restrooms throughout the campground

Difficulty: Easy

Length of Trail: 1 mile Equestrian Loop

Trail Usage: Horseback riding, hiking, mountain biking
Dogs are permitted on a leash.

Directions: Go north out of Ft. Collins on Hwy. 287. Turn west (left) at the Poudre Canyon turnoff Hwy. 14 (Ted's Place). From Ted's Place drive about 24 miles up the canyon to Pingree Park Road. Turn south (left) and drive across the bridge. Travel 6.4 miles to the campground. The campground is on the right side of the road. Continue to day parking or camp overnight.

Camping fee deposited here

Entry to camping area with horses

Camping spot with horse accommodations

Restroom facilities

Day parking as well as trailhead for Little Beaver Creek Trail

General Information: The campground is situated in a large mixed ponderosa pine and aspen stand. There are 71 sites in the campground. Sixty-one sites are suitable for RV camping and 10 are more suitable for tents. Most of the sites are wooded. Each site has a picnic table and fire ring or grate. Some of the sites have electrical hookups. The maximum vehicle length that can be accommodated is 50 feet. The equestrian loop has five sites with four pipe corrals each for camping with your horses. There is also a group camping area available. The roads through the campground are gravel. There are seven water hydrants and six restrooms. In the equestrian campground, there are designated trash bins for horse manure. Reservations are accepted only for the group camping area (970-881-2157 for reservations). This may change in 2005 to allow reservations for all horse camping sites. The season for this campground normally runs from May through mid-November, depending on the weather. At the campground, there is at least one site occupied by the Hosts (look for semi-permanent structures). The Hosts have a phone that can be used for an emergency. A credit card will be needed to make the call. If possible, make contact with the Hosts. There is an "equestrian trail" that runs for about 1 mile round-trip around the equestrian campgrounds. The Flowers, Little Beaver Creek and Fish Creek trails offer great rides for the equestrian and can be started from the campground trailhead. Other trails are available within the Pingree Park area but in most cases, you will need to trailer your horse to the appropriate trailhead. Realize that the trail may change from one ride to the next, due to fallen trees or the maintenance of the trail. During our rides, we found the trails to be minimally marked with signs and somewhat confusing at spots. Some trails could not be found on our map, even though the map was up-to-date. Weed free hay or cubes are required if camping here with your horse.

Notes:

MAP:

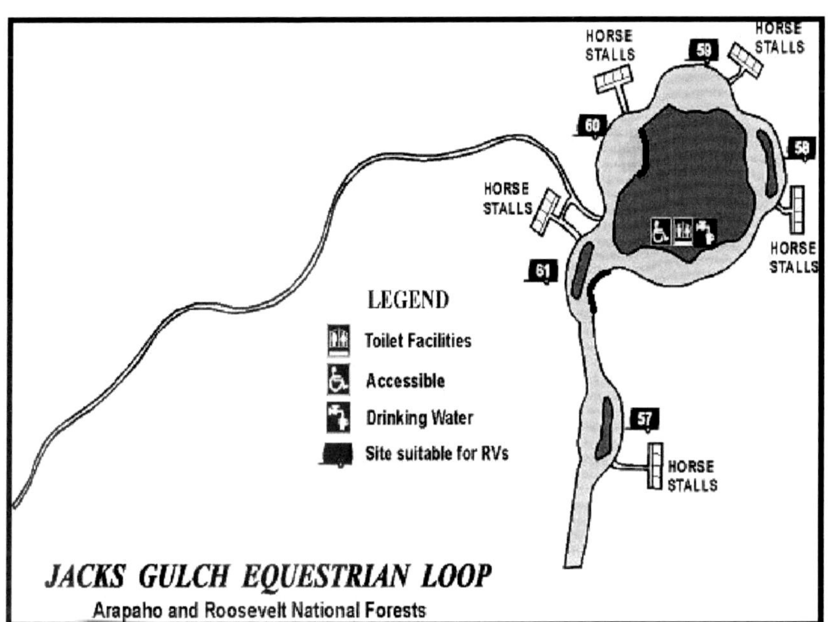

National Geographic Map #112

Trail #15
Trail Name:

Jacks Gulch Circle Trail (Larimer)

Govt. Organization: Arapaho-Roosevelt National Forest

Fees: Yes, call for fees and opening/closing dates (970-498-2770)

Beginning Elevation: 7,900 ft.

Ending Elevation: 8,100 ft.

Trailer Parking: Ample parking for trailers up to 50 feet

Facilities: Six restrooms throughout the campground

Difficulty: Easy to Moderate

Length of Trail: 5 miles round trip

Trail Usage: Horseback riding, hiking, mountain biking
Dogs are permitted on a leash.

Directions: Go north out of Ft. Collins on Hwy. 287. Turn west (left) at the Poudre Canyon turnoff Hwy. 14 (Ted's Place). From Ted's Place drive about 24 miles up the canyon to Pingree Park Road. Turn south (left) and drive across the bridge. Travel 6.4 miles to the campground. The campground is on the right side of the road. Continue to day parking or camp overnight.

Camping at Jacks Gulch

Start of trail was right next to our campsite (#61)

View of meadow from trail

Follow road to the "Y" (see next picture)

At the fork, take the right trail

At the next fork, take the right trail to BedSprings Spring

BedSprings Spring

After backtracking from BedSpring Springs to the fork, take the left trail toward this gate

Continue on trail toward the Aspen grove

Trail meanders through an Aspen grove

Fallen trees across the trail

Trail intersect with Beaver Creek Trail

One last gate to open and close

General Information: This was our first ride at Pingree Park and we almost didn't have the opportunity to experience it. This trail is not on any map or website that we were able to find. As we were setting up camp, we were fortunate to have met other riders who had just finished riding. They told us about the trail, giving us directions as well as landmarks and obstacles that we would encounter, since the trail was unmarked. Without their help, we would have missed out on this excellent ride.

We started from our campsite (Site #61) and rode the ½ mile to the day parking area. Here we picked up the path to the Little Beaver Creek Trail. After going through the gate at the day parking area, be sure to take the trail to the left. At the 1st "Y", take the trail to the right. We took a little detour to BedSprings Spring, by taking a right at the next fork in the road. We rode up to the spring, gave the horses a drink, enjoyed the view, and returned to the fork in the road. At this point we continued up a small hill and approached a small gate. Going through the gate, we rode in a meadow and approached a large stand of Aspen trees. Even in the middle of the summer, it was breathtaking to ride among the Aspen trees. Fallen Aspen trees along the trail did prove to be a slight obstacle. In some places it was impossible to go around the fallen trees and your horse had to go over the trees. Continuing on, the path started down a fairly steep and rocky hillside. At the bottom of the hill, continue riding to the left. Along this portion of the trail, you will be riding with a river (Little Beaver Creek) to your right. The trail gets a little rocky here as well as narrows in spots. Continue on, always taking the trail to the left. You will eventually start to climb slowly up a small grade and will approach a gate. After about another ½ mile, you will encounter the "Y" with the marker "Cutoff Trail." You have now made a complete circle!! Take a right here and continue back to your campsite or your trailer parked at the day parking area.

This would be a awesome ride in the fall!!

Notes:

MAP:

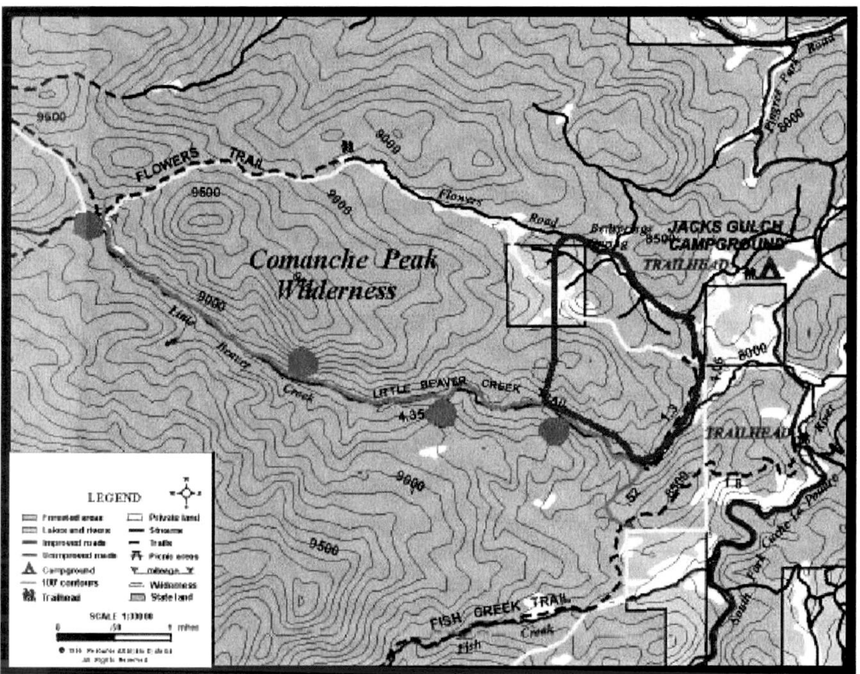

National Geographic Map #112

Trail #16

Trail Name:

Fish Creek Trail (Larimer)

Govt. Organization: Arapaho-Roosevelt National Forest

Fees: None

Beginning Elevation: 7,900 ft.

Ending Elevation: 9,171 ft.

Trailer Parking: Parking is limited to the side of the road.

Facilities: None

Difficulty: Moderate

Length of Trail: 13.2 miles round trip

Trail Usage: Horseback riding, hiking. Dogs are permitted on a leash.

Directions: Go north out of Ft. Collins on Hwy. 287. Turn west (left) at the Poudre Canyon turnoff Hwy. 14 (Ted's Place). From Ted's Place drive about 24 miles up the canyon to Pingree Park Road. Turn south (left) and drive across the bridge. Travel 7.2 miles to the trailhead. This trailhead is approximately 1.5 miles south of the Jack's Gulch Campground. There is another southern trailhead that offers more parking. To get to the south end of the trail, travel an additional 8.3 miles to the Tom Bennett Campground. You can also park at the trailhead at Jacks Gulch and travel along Little Beaver Creek Trail and turn off and connect with Fish Creek Trail.

Trailhead 1.5 miles south of Jack's Gulch Campground

Start of Equestrian Trail at Site #61 at Jack's Gulch

Take the road to the left after going through the gate at the end of the Equestrian Trail at Jack's Gulch Campground

At the fork, take the left trail (Cutoff Trail)

Proceed through the gate

Cross Little Beaver Creek

At the sign for ←Little Beaver Creek→ , take the unmarked trail heading up the mountain

At the top of the trail, turn right. You are now on Fish Creek Trail

Riding along Fish Creek Trail

One of the many meadows along the trail

General Information: We started this trail from the Jacks Gulch campground. We started from our campsite (Site #61) and rode the ½ mile to the day parking area. Here we picked up the path to the Little Beaver Creek Trail. After going through the gate at the day parking area, be sure to take the trail to the left. At the 1st "Y," take the trail to the left (Cutoff Trail). You will proceed down a small hill, over a small creek and through a meadow. Up to this point, the trail is wide and you could ride "side-by-side." Eventually, you will come upon a gate. Proceed through the gate and continue along the trail, climbing a small hill and traveling down the other side. At the bottom of the hill the trail will come to a "Y." Take the left fork toward "Little Beaver Creek." Cross "Little Beaver Creek." In spots, this creek can be deep. My horse tried to jump it (she made it ¾ of the way!!) because where she was going to enter the creek, she couldn't see the bottom. Needless to say, on the return trip, I was aware of the situation and made sure she crossed without jumping. After crossing the creek, continue along the trail. At the sign for ←Little Beaver Creek→, take the unmarked trail heading up the mountain. This is a steady, steep climb and a little rocky. We stopped a few times to let our horses catch their breath. At the top of the trail, turn right. You are now on Fish Creek Trail. From this point on, the trail becomes narrow and winds through several groves of pine trees. Small meadows are inter-dispersed among the stands of trees. Be prepared to do a lot of ducking of branches and taking your foot out of the stirrups in order to clear the trees that cling to the side of the trail. A few times we had to dismount and lead our horse around large trees that had fallen and blocked the trail. The trail follows the north side of Fish Creek and at times is only a few feet away. At about 5.25 miles the trail will cross the creek and make a short climb up the steep hillside out of the drainage. From here it descends slightly to the south trailhead near a church camp. As this trail passes through the Comanche Peak Wilderness, the rules for wilderness travel must be followed. This is an all day ride so expect to be a little sore the next day, especially from weaving back and forth to miss tree branches.

Notes:

MAP:

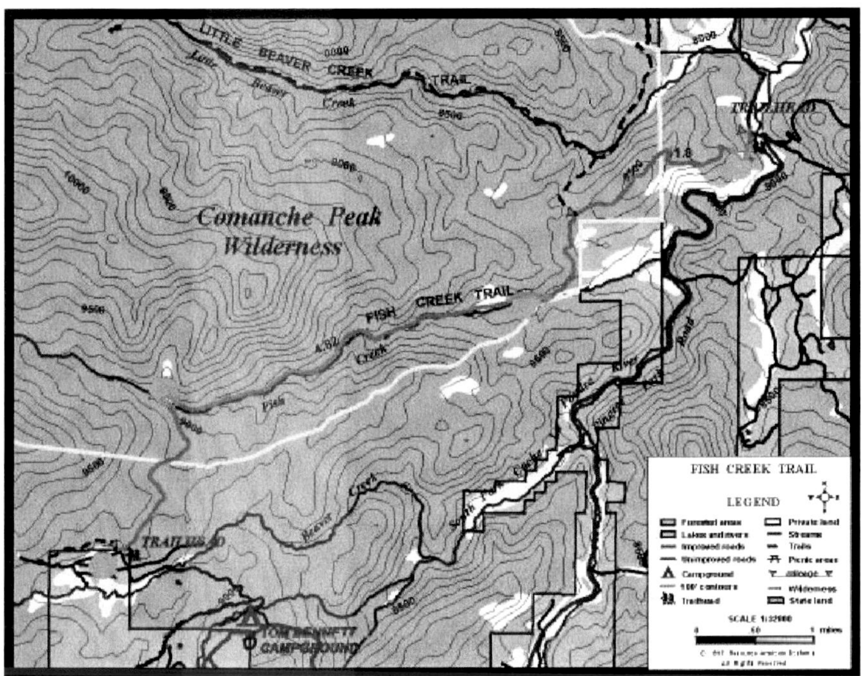

National Geographic Map #112

Trail #17
Trail Name:

Deadman Park (Larimer)

Govt. Organization: Arapaho-Roosevelt National Forest

Fees: None

Beginning Elevation: 10,000 ft.

Ending Elevation: 10,711 ft.

Trailer Parking: Plenty of parking, no designated horse trailer area
Facilities: None at Deadman Park, restrooms at Deadman Lookout (ranger station)

Difficulty: Easy to moderate, depending on trail

Length of Trail: Varies, numerous trails to ride

Trail Usage: Horseback riding, hiking, camping, biking, 4 wheelers. off-road motorcycles. Dogs are permitted on a leash.

Directions: Take Highway 287 north from Ft. Collins to Laporte. Continue on 287 north to Livermore (Forks Cafe). Turn west on 74 E for 27 miles to where the pavement ends. Continue on dirt road, County Road 162 for 11 miles. Here is the turn off for Deadman Lookout. To continue to Deadman Park, travel another 2 miles to mile marker 13. Turn left to Deadman Park, approximately 4 miles down a Level 6 road.

Turnoff at mile marker 13 on Deadman Road

One of the many camping & parking areas available

Another parking area and view of Deadman Park

One of the many valleys around Deadman Park

Parking at Deadman Lookout

View from Deadman Lookout

Restrooms are available at Deadman Lookout

Small Visitor Center at Deadman Lookout

Road to Deadman Lookout

General Information: This is one of the few trails that I have not yet been able to ride my horse on due to bad weather. We did have the opportunity, however, to look around, take some pictures and talk to a few people.

Deadman Park has numerous parking areas where a horse trailer can be parked. Unfortunately, it is not set up like Jacks Gulch, so you will have to bring portable horse panels with you if you would like to camp with your horses. There are numerous streams nearby providing water for your horse, but you will have to bring in water for yourself. Weed free hay or cubes is a must for your horse. At the time that we visited, the large meadow was fenced off to all activities. Do not despair; there are plenty of roads branching off of Deadman Park road for horseback riding. This area seemed to be popular with ATVs.

An excellent ride would be from Deadman Park to Deadman Lookout and back, approximately 12 miles round trip. The ride would be on wide, dirt roads. The road to Deadman Lookout is lined on both sides by large trees. The views from Deadman Lookout are spectacular.

The Killpecker trail would be another trail available if camping at Deadman Park.

Deadman Park and Deadman Lookout are on the top of my list for a summer ride.

Notes:

MAP:

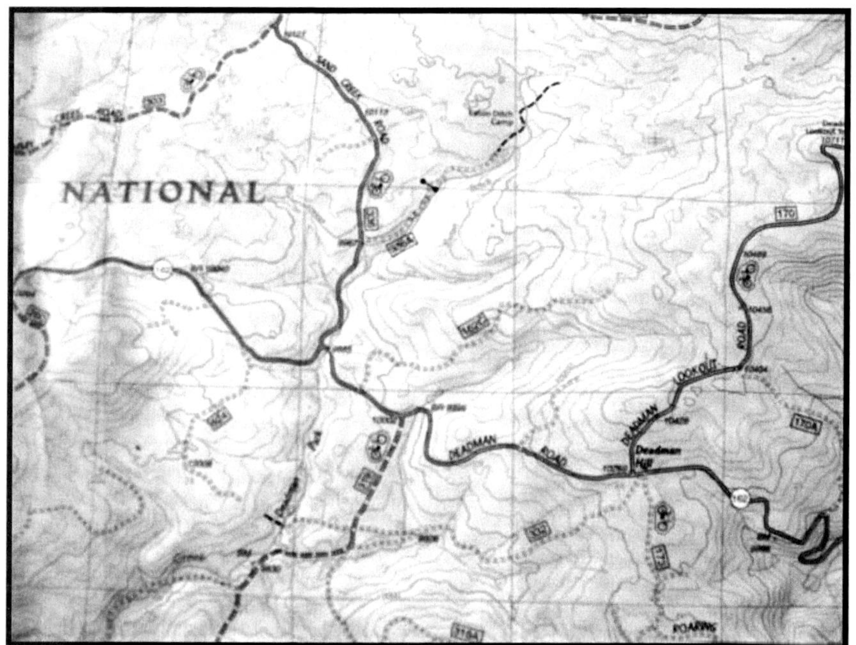

National Geographic Map #111

Trail #18
Trail Name:

Mount Margaret (Larimer)

Govt. Organization: Arapaho-Roosevelt National Forest

Fees: None

Beginning Elevation: 7,904 ft.

Ending Elevation: 8,143 ft.

Trailer Parking: Plenty of parking, no designated horse trailer area. Additional parking is available 1 mile further west on left side of road. Well-known trail and the parking can become limited.

Facilities: None

Difficulty: Easy

Length of Trail: 11 miles if A Loop (1.5 mi) and B Loop (1.5 mi) are ridden

Trail Usage: Horseback riding, hiking, camping, biking. Dogs are permitted on a leash.

Directions: Take Highway 287 north from Ft. Collins to Laporte. Continue on 287 north to Livermore (Forks Café). Turn west on 74E for 22 miles to the trailhead. The trailhead is on the north side (right side) of the highway. Be careful, it's easy to miss the turn off. There is no advance warning such as a sign marking the trailhead. If you miss it, you can continue another 1 mile and there is another trailhead on the left. If you use this parking area, it will add an additional 2 miles and you will have to cross 74E to get to the main trailhead.

Parking at Trailhead #1

Parking at Trailhead #2

Gate at the main trailhead

98% of the trail is wide enough for "side-by-side" riding

One stream crossing at beginning of trail
Expect to encounter cattle

One more gate to open and close

Along the way, the trail may fork off to Dowdy Lake or make loops (A Loop and B Loop) with the main trail

Trail winds through a stand of aspens

Trail is very well marked

Last 5 % of trail will be a little rocky with riding "head to tail"

View near end of trail

Summit Marker

General Information: What a fantastic trail!! If you are looking for a trail that is easy and relaxing, this is it. The trail is fairly level and winds through many large open meadows and stands of aspen and ponderosa trees. Many large beautiful rock formations can be seen on either side of the trail. The majority of the trail follows an old road bed, allowing you to ride "side-by-side." There is one water crossing at the beginning of the trail and there is a very good possibility of sharing the crossing with cattle. Expect to see hikers and mountain bikes as well as campers along the way, especially on the weekends. Several side trails lead to Dowdy Lake as well as loops (A Loop and B Loop) that join up with the main trail. We took the loops and enjoyed them tremendously. We rode during the week and saw very few people which allowed us to canter our horses in a few spots. The last 1 ½ miles becomes a little narrow with a few rocky spots, making you ride "head to tail." The climb is gradual and very small, but the views are awesome. This is another trail well suited for a green horse, your first ride of the summer or as I stated earlier, just a relaxing ride. Be aware that this is a well known trail and is used regularly, especially on the weekends.

If you park a mile further up on the south side (left side) of 74E (trailhead #2), you will have to cross the highway to get to the main trailhead. This would give you 2 additional miles round trip that is also very relaxing and beautiful.

Notes:

MAP:

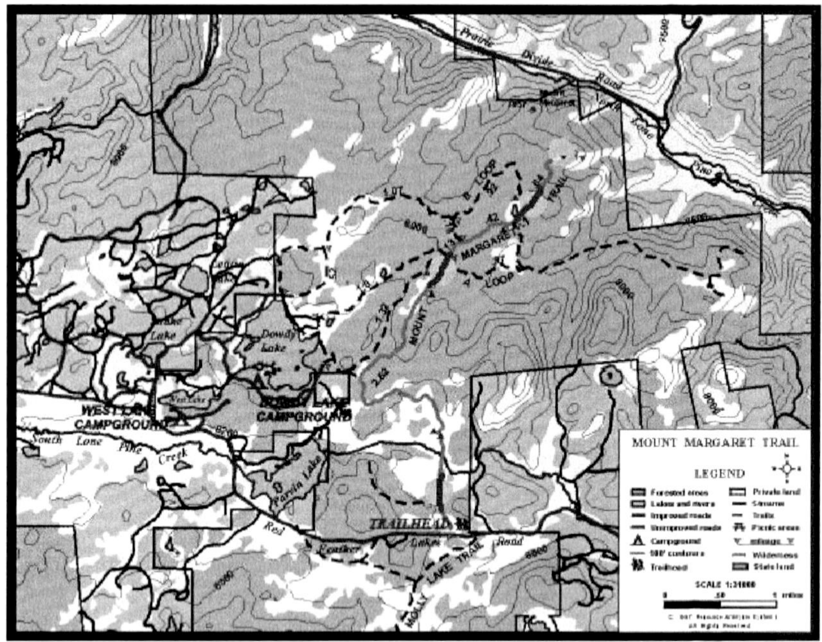

National Geographic Map #111

Trail #19
Trail Name:

Molly Lake (Larimer)

Govt. Organization: Arapaho-Roosevelt National Forest

Fees: None

Beginning Elevation: 8,038 ft.

Ending Elevation: 8,624 ft.

Trailer Parking: Plenty of parking, no designated horse trailer area. Multiple trailheads can be used.

Facilities: None. Water is not available for your horse along the trail.

Difficulty: Easy

Length of Trail: 10 to 12 miles roundtrip depending on trailhead used

Trail Usage: Horseback riding, hiking, Dogs are permitted on a leash.

Directions: Take Highway 287 north from Ft. Collins to Laporte. Continue on 287 north to Livermore (Forks Café). Turn west on 74E for 22 miles to the trailhead. The trailhead (#1) is on the north side (right side) of the highway. Be careful, it's easy to miss the turn off. There is no advance warning such as a sign marking the trailhead. If you miss it, you can continue another 1 mile and there is another trailhead (#2) on the south side (left. side). Trailhead #3 is 27 miles on 74E. Turn south (left) on County Road 162 (Manhatten Road) and go 2.3 miles to the trailhead. The trailhead is on the left side of the road.

Parking at Trailhead #1

Parking at Trailhead #2

After going through a small gate, a narrow trail heads toward a meadow

Turn left (east) at this post

Trail heads east and skirts a large meadow to the south

Trail continues through a "collapsible barbed wire" gate

At this crossroad, take a right (south) toward Molly Lake Trailhead

Trail widens and follows an old roadbed.

Small bog you need to cross

Trail is well marked

Other riders enjoying a fall ride

Take left (west) fork in road toward Molly Lake Trailhead

Talking with other users of the trail

Small gate right after turning west at fork

Continuing to steadily climb toward the summit of the trail

Trail winds through rock formations and stands of aspen and pine

Trail gets a little rocky on the other side of the summit

Approaching a gate

Sign on west side of gate

Continuing west on trail and another gate to open/close

Division of Wildlife personnel that we met along the way

General Information: We parked and started this trail at Trailhead #2. The trail starts at the Southwest end of the parking area after you pass through a small gate. At the bottom of a small grade you will encounter a post without a sign at an intersection. Take the left fork (east) through some pine trees with a large meadow on your right. At approximately one mile, you will ride through a "collapsible barbed wire" gate and come to an intersection. Take the right fork and head south (if you turn left, you will ride to County Rd 74E with the Mt. Margaret trailhead across the road.). The trail becomes an old roadbed that is sandy and well drained. Not far from this intersection, at the time that we rode, there was a small bog that we had to cross. This bog may or may not exist when you ride; depending upon the amount of precipitation the area has received. The trail will then start to climb gradually to where you will come to another intersection. Here you will take a right (west) toward the Molly Lake Trailhead (if you turn left, you will be going toward Lady Moon Lake). Proceed through a small gate and continue your gradual climb through forests of aspens, lodgepole pine and ponderosa pine. All along the ride, we saw elk and deer tracks. We encountered the only small stretch of rocky trail after we rode over the summit. As we descended, we came upon another gate. On the other side of the gate was a sign with markings for Redfeather Lake Road and Elkhorn Cr. Continue to ride west toward the Molly Lake Trailhead where you will come upon another gate. Pass through the gate and travel a short distance. Another sign post will be marked informing you to be .9 miles from the Molly Lake Trailhead. We expected to be able to see Molly Lake from this trail, but found that the lake is a short walk north of the trail about a mile from the Molly Lake Trailhead at Manhattan Road (trailhead #3).

This trail can be busy with hikers as well as horseback riders. Our ride was relaxing, with breathtaking views. I would suggest that you bring along water for your horse after the ride as well as packing a lunch for yourself. Because this is a long ride, I would start early and make sure that your horse is in good physical condition.

Notes:

MAP:

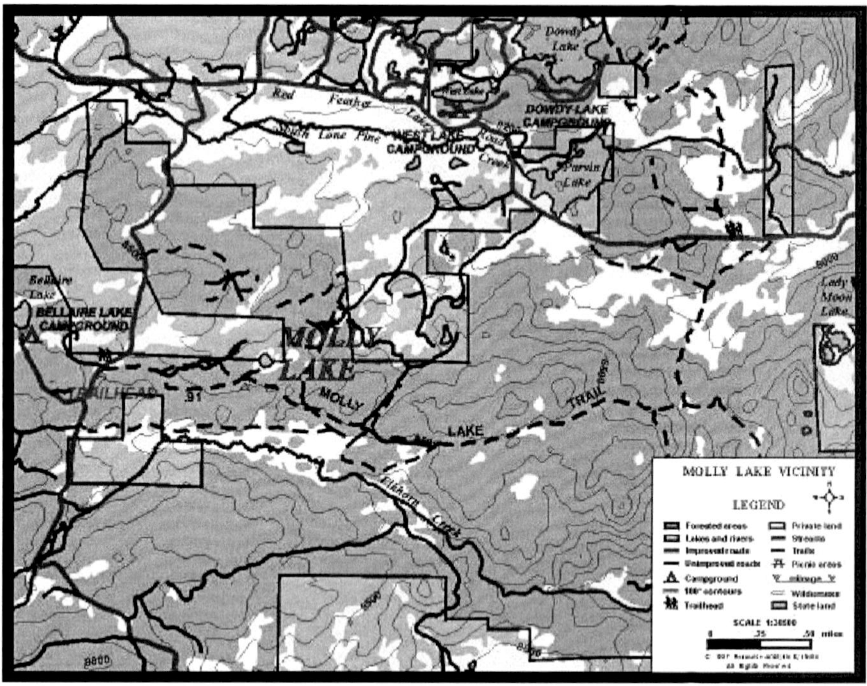

National Geographic Map #111

Trail #20

Trail Name:

Pawnee National Grassland (Weld)

Govt. Organization: Arapaho-Roosevelt National Forest

Fees: None

Beginning Elevation: 4,900 ft. on the prairie

Ending Elevation: 5,500 ft. at the summit of the Pawnee Buttes

Trailer Parking: Parking is limited to parking within 300 feet off the numbered roads for horse trailers. See map on page 184 for favorite unloading sites.

Facilities: None. During the summer, the wells are running and water is available from the stock tanks for your horses.

Difficulty: Easy to moderate.

Length of Trail: 193,000 acres

Trail Usage: Horseback riding, hiking, camping, biking, and picnics. Dogs are permitted on a leash.

Directions: Because the Pawnee National Grassland is contained within a 30 by 60 mile area, interspersed with private land, it is impossible to give detailed directions here. Before traveling on the Pawnee National Grassland, I recommend purchasing a Grassland map to help you to distinguish between public lands and private ownership. The cost is $6.00 each. The maps are available at the Greeley office at 660 O Street, Greeley, Colorado 80631 (970) 353-5004

General Information: The Pawnee is an internationally known birding area. The Colorado State Bird, the lark bunting, as well as the mountain plover, burrowing owl and various birds of prey are found on the grassland. Riding horses across the fairly level, open prairie has become an increasing popular activity. Most of the riding is done cross-country. Be aware that the grassland is criss-crossed by many steep ravines. There is only one developed trail; the Pawnee Buttes (see trail information). Horses are not permitted in the Crow Valley Recreation Area (campground) and trailers cannot be parked and unloaded there. Again, a map is highly recommended.

Any feed you bring along must either be processed (ex. alfalfa cubes) or certified weed free. During the summer the windmills are running and water is available from the stock tanks. In the winter the windmills are turned off, so it will be necessary to bring water for your horses. If you are camping on the prairie, you may picket your horses. Do "not" tie animals to a live tree. Sun screen, water, hat and sunglasses are necessary items, especially during the hotter months. Leather gloves would be helpful in opening/closing the barb wire gates. Watch the weather closely for sudden thunderstorms with strong winds are common in this area. Remember, there is very little protection on the prairie and many roads can become impassable when wet. Be wary of where you step, rattlesnakes are very common on the grassland. Riding your horse on the Pawnee National Grassland is like stepping back in time. Experience the abundant wildlife and peaceful serenity and let your imagination run free.

Notes:

MAP:

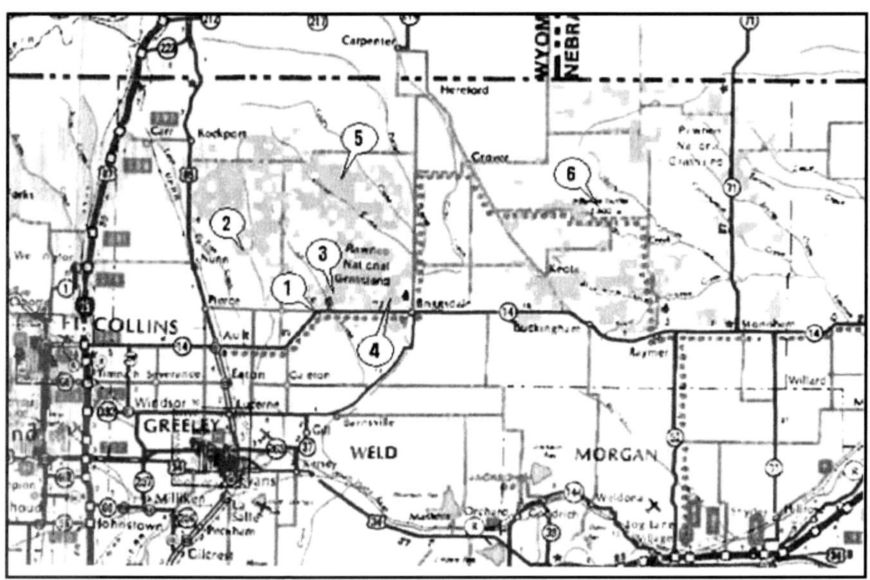

This map does NOT show county roads or private land boundaries. Use this map to determine general locations only!

Favorite unloading sites as shown on above map:

1	**At the intersection of Hwy. 14 and Weld County Road 57. Approximately 22 miles north of Greeley.**
2	**Just north of intersection of Weld County Roads 102 and 41. Approximately 24 miles northeast of Greeley.**
3	**At the intersection of Weld County Roads 96 and 61. Approximately 27 miles northeast of Greeley.**
4	**Forest Service Road 607. 30.5 miles northeast of Greeley, just north of Hwy 14.**
5	**One mile east of intersection of Weld County Roads 120 and 59. Approximately 39 miles northeast of Greeley.**
6	**Pawnee Buttes Trail, 60 miles northeast of Greeley**

Trail #21
Trail Name:

Pawnee Buttes Trail (Weld)

Govt. Organization: Arapaho-Roosevelt National Forest

Fees: None

Beginning Elevation: 4,900 ft. on the prairie

Ending Elevation: 5,500 ft. at the summit of the Pawnee Buttes

Trailer Parking: Parking easily accommodates large trailers with ample room to navigate. Parking is limited to parking within 300 feet off the numbered roads for horse trailers.

Facilities: None. During the summer, the wells are running and water is available from the stock tanks for your horses.

Difficulty: Easy

Length of Trail: 3 miles roundtrip One portion of the trail is closed due to nesting birds from March through June.

Trail Usage: Horseback riding, hiking. Dogs are permitted on a leash.

Directions: From Ft. Collins, drive 45 miles east on Highway 14. After passing the Briggsdale exit (County Road 77), continue for another 13 miles and turn north (left) toward the town of Keota on CountyRroad 103. Drive 4.5 miles north on County Road 103 to Keota. At Keota, continue north on County Road 105 for 3 miles. Turn east (right) on County Road 104 and drive 3 miles. Turn north (left) on County Road 111 and drive 4.5 miles to where a secondary road turns north. Follow this road for less than a mile to the signed trailhead.

Turn north at the "Y" to the trailhead

Parking Area and Corral

Water south of Parking Area

Trailhead to West Butte

Entry to the Buttes

Sandstone bluffs line both sides at the beginning of the trail

Pawnee Buttes

Pawnee Buttes

Various sections of the path have been shored up with timbers

Trail closed, nesting birds March through June

Private land intermingles with public land

General Information: The trail begins by dropping easily from the trailhead into a broad drainage. The trail is well worn and easy to follow. Timbers and paving stones have been used on various sections of the trail to help deter erosion. Near the drainage bottom, the trail passes through a gate in the fence and continues north through another drainage. Low sandstone bluffs line both sides of the trail. These areas are off limits from March 1st to June 30 to protect nesting birds of prey (prairie falcons, golden eagles and hawks). The trail will continue to wind its way through another shallow drainage, flanked by scattered juniper, prickly pear cactus and yucca. From this point on, the trail lacks any means for shade. During July and August, temperatures of over 100 degrees can be encountered. Make sure you have a hat, sunscreen lotion and water. The trail continues east toward the bluffs, where you will notice "private land" signs. Respect the rights of the private property owners in the area and stay on the trail. At the end of the trail, turn around and retrace your steps back to the trailhead. Keep your eye on the weather and watch out for flash floods in the wash bottoms. As this area is known for rattlesnakes, be wary especially when exploring the public land off of the established trail. The area can also be very windy. It would be a good idea to call the Visitor Information line at (970) 353-5004 Monday – Friday: 8-4:30 prior to planning a ride.

Notes:

MAP:

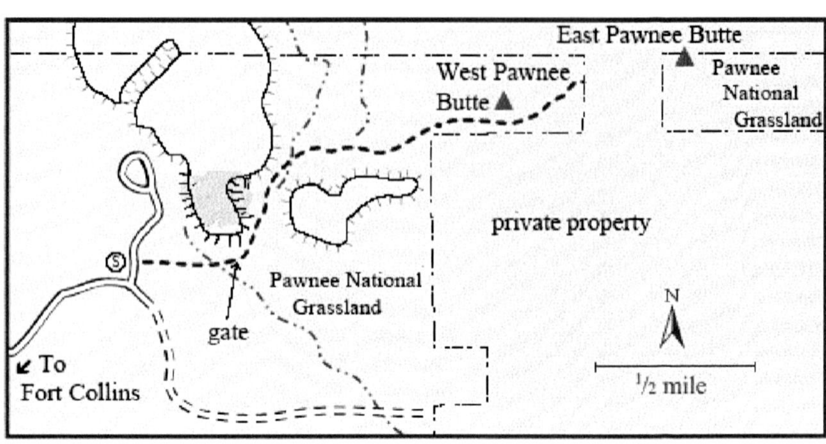
East Pawnee Butte
West Pawnee
Butte
Pawnee
National
Grassland
private property
S
gate
Pawnee National
Grassland
N
To
Fort Collins
½ mile

Trail #22
Trail Name:

Bonny Lake State Park (Yuma)

Govt. Organization: Colorado Sate Parks

Fees: Yes, As of this writing Daily Fee $5, Annual pass $55

Beginning Elevation: 3,700 ft.

Ending Elevation: 3,700 ft.

Trailer Parking: Available at Foster Grove camp sites

Facilities: Water and restrooms located at various spots in park

Difficulty: Easy

Length of Trail: Varies, park covers a vast area as well as borders Department of Wildlife areas

Trail Usage: Horseback riding, hiking. Dogs are permitted on a leash.

Directions: From Denver: Take I-70 east to Burlington, then 23 miles north on U.S. 385. Turn east on County Road 2 (3 1\2 miles to gate entrance) or County Road 3 (1 1\2 miles to gate entrance.)

OR

Take I-70 east to Byers, then east on U.S. 36 (approximately 108 miles) to Idalia. Continue east two miles on U.S. 36, then turn south on U.S. 385 for 6 or 7 miles to County Road 2 (3 1\2 miles to gate entrance) or County Road 3 (1 1\2 miles to gate entrance.)

From Northern Colorado: Take Hwy. 14 east to Wray, Colorado. Turn south on U.S. 385. Proceed south. Bonny Lake Park is 23 miles north of Burlington

Park Headquarters

Sample of one of the many roads within the park

Sunset along the lake

General Information: Bonny Lake offers excellent camping, horseback riding, hunting and fishing. The park is also well known as a spring and summer water-sports area for fishing, boating and other water sports. The park is open year round allowing for winter riding. Bonny Lake State Park has four campgrounds with 190 campsites. Campers with horses are to use the Foster Grove campsite only. There are no special accommodations for horses. It is recommended that you bring your own portable panels for your horses. Horseback riding is allowed on all surrounding roads and within the park as well as on grassy areas. Horseback riding is "not" allowed on the Nature Trail, among the other campground areas (North Cove, East Beach or Wagon Wheel) and along the east and west Beaches. Department of Wildlife (DOW) land borders much of Bonny Lake Park. A map is available from the park headquarters outlining any block out dates for horseback riding on these properties. If it is your first visit to Bonny Lake Park, I suggest that you stop and visit the park headquarters to get your daily park and camping pass. During hunting season be sure to outfit yourself and your horse in hunter orange. Reservations are encouraged for weekends and holidays. For reservations call 1-800-678-CAMP (2267). Bonny Lake State Park has something for everyone, whether you ride horses or not. We found this Eastern Colorado State Park to be a pleasant surprise.

Notes:

MAP:

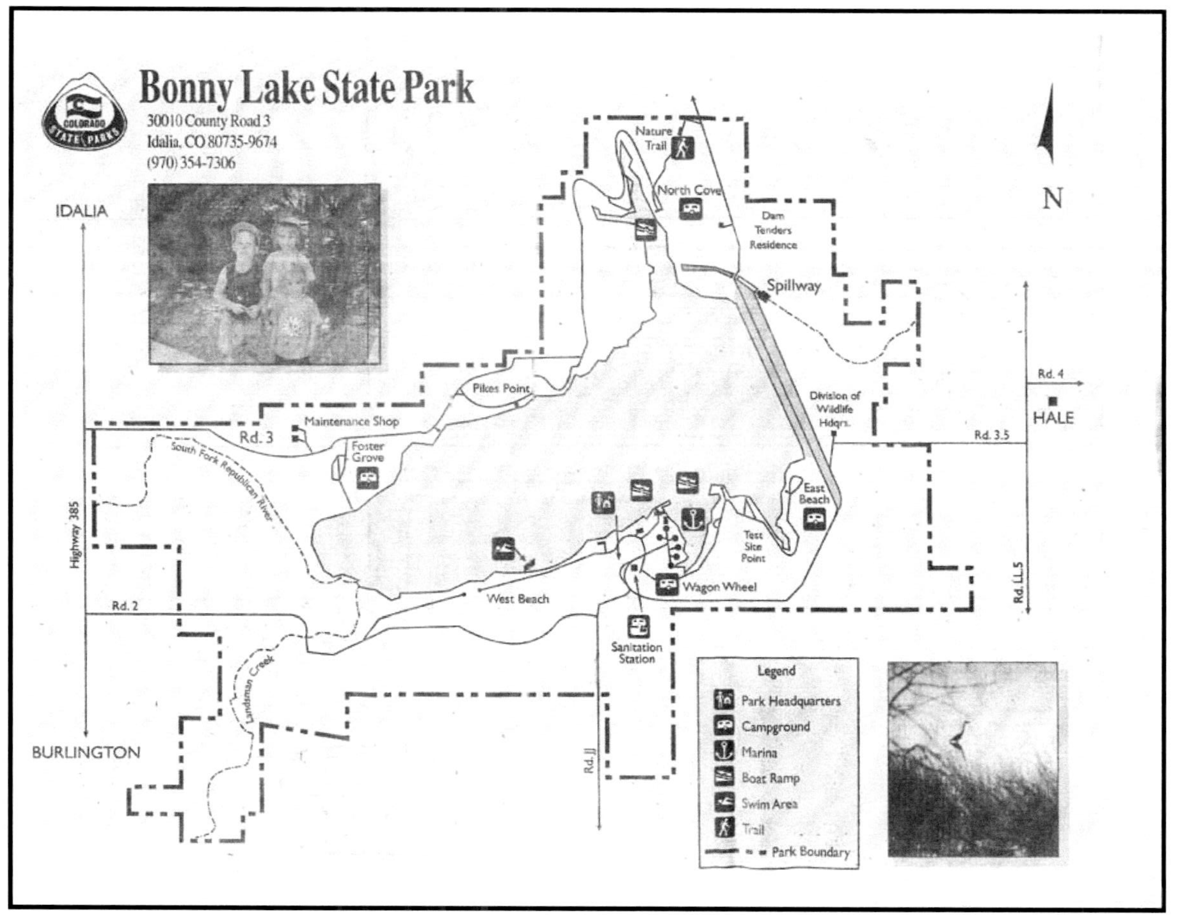

Bonny Lake State Park
30010 County Road 3
Idalia, CO 80735-9674
(970) 354-7306
COLORADO STATE PARKS
N
IDALIA
BURLINGTON
Highway 385
Rd. 2
Rd. 3
South Fork Republican River
Landsman Creek
Maintenance Shop
Foster Grove
Pikes Point
Nature Trail
North Cove
Dam Tenders Residence
Spillway
Division of Wildlife Hdqrs.
Rd. 4
HALE
Rd. 3.5
Rd. LL.5
East Beach
Test Site Point
Wagon Wheel
West Beach
Sanitation Station
Rd. JJ
Legend
Park Headquarters
Campground
Marina
Boat Ramp
Swim Area
Trail
Park Boundary

Suggested Articles to Take On Your Ride

- EasyBoot(s)
- Hoof Pick
- Vet Wrap
- Small First Aid Kit (people and horse items)
- Water Bottle(s)
- Plastic tube(s) (approx ¾ inch in diameter) (If your horse was bitten by a rattlesnake on the nose, these are inserted into the horse's nose to allow your horse to breath)
- Sun Block
- Chap Stick
- Wrap around Sun Glasses (Protects your eyes from the wind and the sun as well as low hanging tree branches)
- Leather Shoe Laces (I have used laces to replace Chicago screws that have fallen out of my headstall)
- Cell Phone (Even though cell phone service may not be available in all areas, this is still a good item to carry)
- Binoculars
- Compass/GPS unit
- Map of area with trails if available
- People Snacks
- Leatherman (For cutting shoe laces, wire, tighten Chicago screws, etc.)
- Raincoat (It should be long enough to cover your saddle)
- Toilet Paper/Tissues
- Leather gloves (Helps when opening tight barb wire gates)
- Camera (Not a necessity, but nice to have)
- Waterproof matches
- Halter and lead rope (I usually ride with this under my bridle with the end of my lead rope tied to my saddle)
- Large bells to tie to saddle or breast collar (The noise will let anyone or anything know that you are on the trail)
- Leg wraps for your horse
- Pepper Spray
- Chaps

Suggested Extra Tack and Miscellaneous Items for Your Horse Trailer

- Saddle Blanket
- Bridle
- Halter
- Lead Rope
- Girth Strap
- Bug Spray for you and your horse
- Various Horse Brushes
- Jacket/Sweatshirt/Sweater (In the mountains during the summer, snow is not uncommon)
- Orange vest for riding during hunting season
- Leather Work Gloves
- Winter Gloves
- Star Nut Wrench (Check to make sure the wrench fits your lug nuts on the horse trailer as well as your towing vehicle)
- Jack for the horse trailer (The type you drive up on is the easiest)
- WD40 (I've used this to loosen the lug nuts)
- Large First Aid Kit
- Can with lid containing oats (If your horse should get loose, rattling a can with oats might help to get him/her back)
- Emergency Phone numbers and/or local phone book
- Couple gallons of water (We use 6 gallon containers)
- Water Bucket
- Rake
- Horse blanket
- Small wheelbarrow (If camping, this is good for carrying water for your horses as well as clean-up of manure)
- Copy of your horse's Brand Inspection
- Battery operated radio

Why Your Horse May Be Sore After Trimming

by John Hunter, Professional Farrier

As you are reading this, the hooves of your horse are growing. Even as your Farrier is trimming them they are growing. And as they are growing, they are growing out of balance. Out of balance means that the hoof isn't hitting the ground flat. If it isn't landing flat then some portion of the hoof is being subjected to excessive stresses and forces that are causing harm. In all likelihood the toe is becoming longer and the heels are hitting the ground first, causing them to be pushed forward giving the hoof the appearance of having no heel at all. The forces coming down from above are now concentrated on the rear most portion of the hoof. The Deep Flexor Tendon is being stretched more and more and the Superficial Tendon at the front of the hoof is doing less and less work. If this process continues for too long, then the onset of Navicular Lameness has begun and the likelihood of pulling a tendon is very high. Both of these are serious and could cause you lots of missed riding time and in many cases the loss of your horse. "FOOD FOR THOUGHT."

Now along comes your Farrier and trims the hoof back into balance, although many times this can't be done, simply because its been far too long since the last trim was done. In such cases the use of a wedge pad is necessary to achieve a correct state of balance; more expense for you.

If the hoof has been balanced correctly then the aforementioned process of excessive stresses on the tendons has been reversed. The front tendon is now working as it should and will be sore for a day or two. This soreness has nothing to do with removing too much sole. Removal of excessive growth of sole and frog is absolutely necessary when dealing with neglected and improperly cared for hooves.

Why Your Horse May Be Sore After Trimming
(Continued)

Therefore, it is to everyone's benefit to keep your horse on a regular program of hoof care [not to exceed 8 weeks between farrier visits] by an experienced and skilled farrier. If you have to have serious corrective work done on the hooves then the money you thought you were saving by not having the hooves trimmed regularly will have been wiped out many times over.

Example: Bar Shoes: $150 minimum.
Wedge Pads: $ 30 minimum
X-rays: Probably $100 at least.

And this is for just the first time. If this has to be done for a lengthy period [6 months to a year for a pulled tendon] then the cost will begin to really add up. "MORE FOOD FOR THOUGHT."
To prevent your horse from becoming sore after each trimming, keep it on a regular schedule not to exceed 8 weeks between farrier visits.

Why Equine Massage

by Shannon K Bryant, Equitouch ® Certified Bodyworker

A horse uses a multitude of muscles to move itself forward, backward and laterally during eventing, pleasure riding and everyday activities. Stresses are put on these muscles and left unchecked can cause discomfort, tension and pain for your horse. These can lead to anxiety, lack of willingness to perform and change in temperament.

Therapeutic massage has become a means to relieve this stress on the muscle tissue when it becomes tight and knotted from overuse and overstretching. Restricted motion occurs when a muscle cannot fully contract or fully release from contraction which affects the horse's fitness performance. As circulation becomes impaired, healing cannot take place efficiently and performance may not be at the expected level.

Massage helps blood and lymph circulation and releases muscles from spasm. Anxiety and fatigue can be reduced through the proper use of massage techniques. Sports massage "pre" and "post" event is used as a preventative for severe muscle strain or injury. When an injury does occur your veterinarian will determine what application of massage will help speed the natural healing process.

Under the supervision of a veterinarian, therapeutic massage may also benefit mares during pregnancy for comfort, relaxation and blood and lymph circulation.

Conditions and Results

Different activities affect different areas of the horse more frequently, but there are sections that are affected in almost every arena.

Western events such as *–Barrel racing/Pole Bending/Calf Roping/Reining:* gluteals, semitendinosus & biceps femoris (hamstrings), triceps, latissismus dorsi, rotator cuff, trapezius C/T, deltoid, brachiocephalicus, rhomboid C/T, these sports put a great deal of pressure on the hocks and other joints. Therapeutic massage includes massaging these areas for circulation.

English events such as *–Dressage/Hunter-Under-Saddle/Hunter Hack/Hunter:* jumping puts a great deal of pressure on the semitendinosus & biceps femoris (hamstrings), gluteals, abdominals, latissimus dorsi, triceps, biceps brachii, brachiophalicus, rotator cuff & serratuts ventralis. Dressage causes tension to form in the rhomboids, splenius, serratus ventralis, lower brachiocephalicus, rotator cuff, pectorals, triceps, trapezius C/T, abdominals & latissimus dorsi. The half pass, pirouette, piaffe and even flying changes cause special tension on the muscles.

Hunter-Under-Saddle/Western Pleasure/Pleasure Riding: all other activities still require movement of the horse and can cause muscle strain in various locations. Tripping during arena or trail riding causes muscle to tense, working after an extended period of rest can cause sore and tired muscles. Tense, strained, knotted muscles prevent your horse from performing at his/her top level. Regular massage will keep those muscles supple, conditioned and relaxed.

Pastured/Stalled Horses: Stalled horses benefit from massage to increase blood circulation to prevent muscle tension and stiffness. If they are there due to illness or injury, massage under veterinary direction can help the healing process and keep the horse relaxed and stress-free. Pastured horses have the potential to strain, stress or injure themselves during play, grazing, or (I've found) just standing still. Regular massage is a way to spot treat these stresses before they become problems or in other cases discover a situation that needs to be treated by the veterinarian.

Conclusions

Therapeutic massage administered regularly, in conjunction with good veterinary care, regular farrier visits, chiropractic work and dental management can provide you with a lifelong, well-balanced partner in your horse

Additional Local Information

Local Farriers

John Hunter
(970) 231-7360

Randy Stephens
(970) 532-5707

Local Veterinarians

Susan J. Williams, DVM
(970) 461-2061

Fossil Creek Veterinary Hospital
(970) 204-1663

Colorado State University-Veterinary
(970) 221-4535

Laporte Animal Clinic & Supply
(970) 490-1999

Ben D. Brown (Cornish Vet Service)
(970) 351-6752 – Office
(970) 590-4933 - Mobile
(970) 356-8358 - Pager

Local Feed & Tack Stores

Ranch-Way Feeds
(970) 482-1662

Loveland Saddle & Tack
(970) 663-0559

Jax Farm & Ranch
(970) 484-2221

287 Supply
(970) 493-7322

Westside Feed
(970) 622-8658

Poudre Pet & Feed Supply
(970) 484-2461 or (970) 225-1255

Murdoch's Ranch & Supply
Cheyenne, WY
(307) 632-7888

Murdoch's Ranch & Supply
Longmont
(303) 682-5111

Hygiene Feed & Supply
(303) 776-4757

Lafayette Feed & Grain
(303) 665-5055

Nightwinds Tack Shop, Inc.
(970) 532-2463

Happy Horse Tack & Saddle Shop
(970) 484-4199

Vetline
(970) 484-1900

Fourwinds
(970) 482-0767

Additional Local Information
(Continued)

Bed & Breakfast with horse facilities

West Pawnee Ranch Bed & Breakfast
29451 Weld County Road 130
Grover, Co 80729
(970) 895-2482

Sundance Trail Guest Ranch
17931 Red Feather Lakes Rd
Red Feather Lakes, Co 80545
(970) 224-1222

Short Term Overnight Boarding

Rockn'R ~ King Ranch Equine Center
2517 S. County Rd 29
Loveland, Co 80537
(970) 613-9287

Sun Pony Ranch
WCR1
Berthoud, Co
(970) 532-4040

Calico Stables
3204 South County Road 21
Loveland, Co
(970) 219-6060

Colorado Division of Wildlife

DOW Headquarters
6060 Broadway
Denver, Co 80216
(303) 297-1192

Ft. Collins Service Center
317 W. Prospect
Ft. Collins, Co 80536
(970) 472-4300

Certified Weed-Free Hay or Cubes

Suppliers
Ranch-Way Feeds
546 Willow
Ft. Collins, Co
(970) 493-7322

Northern Colorado Feeder Supply
359 Linden
Ft. Collins, Co
(970) 482-7303

Poudre Pet & Feed Supply
6204 S. College
Ft. Collins, Co
(970) 225-1255

287 Supply
120 N. Hwy 287
Ft. Collins, Co
(970) 493-7322

Weed-Free Hay Producers are listed by:
Colorado Department of Agriculture
Division of Plant Industry
Lakewood, Co 80215
(303)239-4149
www.ag.state.co.us/dpi
Click weed-free forage

Acknowledgements

Writing this book has been one of my most rewarding experiences. I have seen many beautiful sites, met many interesting people and most of all, I have spent many enjoyable hours on horseback. Without my horse and partner "Gem" (Shawnee's Irish Gem), as well as my friend and riding partner, Mary and her horse "Sonny," this book would just be a dream of mine. I'm grateful for the encouragement my husband, Will, gave me along the way. His suggestions and proof reading was extremely appreciated and valued. To my farrier, John Hunter, thank you for keeping my horse well shod as well as the excellent article on hoof care. Last but not least, a hearty "Thank You" to my Grandson, Seth, who hiked many miles of trails with me and had the blisters to prove it!!

I hope this book will lead you and your horse to many memorable rides. Keep a lookout for the next book in the series due out in the Fall of 2005:

Horse Trails of "Colorful" Colorado

Central Colorado– Book 1

(Contains trails from Boulder, Douglas, Adam, Arapahoe & nearby counties)

Check out the website for upcoming events at
www.horsebacktrails.com

Contact me with feedback at **horsebacktrails@yahoo.com**

Or

Ride The Western Trails Publications
2204 Eagle Drive
Loveland, Colorado 80537

NOTES

Complete Your Ride!

When you hit the trails for a ride in Northern Colorado, take along Ranch-Way Feeds' ***All★American Complete Horse.*** ***Complete Horse*** *is a pelleted ration that provides all the protein, energy, roughage, vitamins and minerals that adult horses require.* ***Complete Horse*** *is certified weed free and may be used for pack trips into National Forests, State Parks and National Parks.* ***Complete Horse*** *is 13% Protein, 3% Fat, and 18% Fiber.* ***Complete Horse Feed*** *contains Chelated Trace Minerals, Yeast Culture, Yucca and Biotin.*

All★American Complete Horse **is available throughout Northern Colorado at Ranch-Way Feeds dealers.**

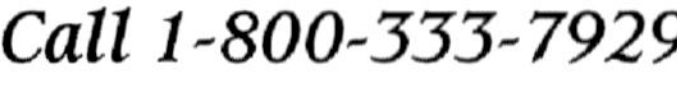

546 Willow Street,
Downtown Fort Collins
970-482-1662
7 to 5:30 Monday thru Friday
7:30 to Noon on Saturday • Closed Sunday

Scott Murdock Trailer Sales

Loveland and Grand Junction, CO
Contact us @ (800) 688-8757 or
e-mail at olemurdock@aol.com

Designed by "Ride The Western Trails Publications"

The Card Corral

The Card Corral

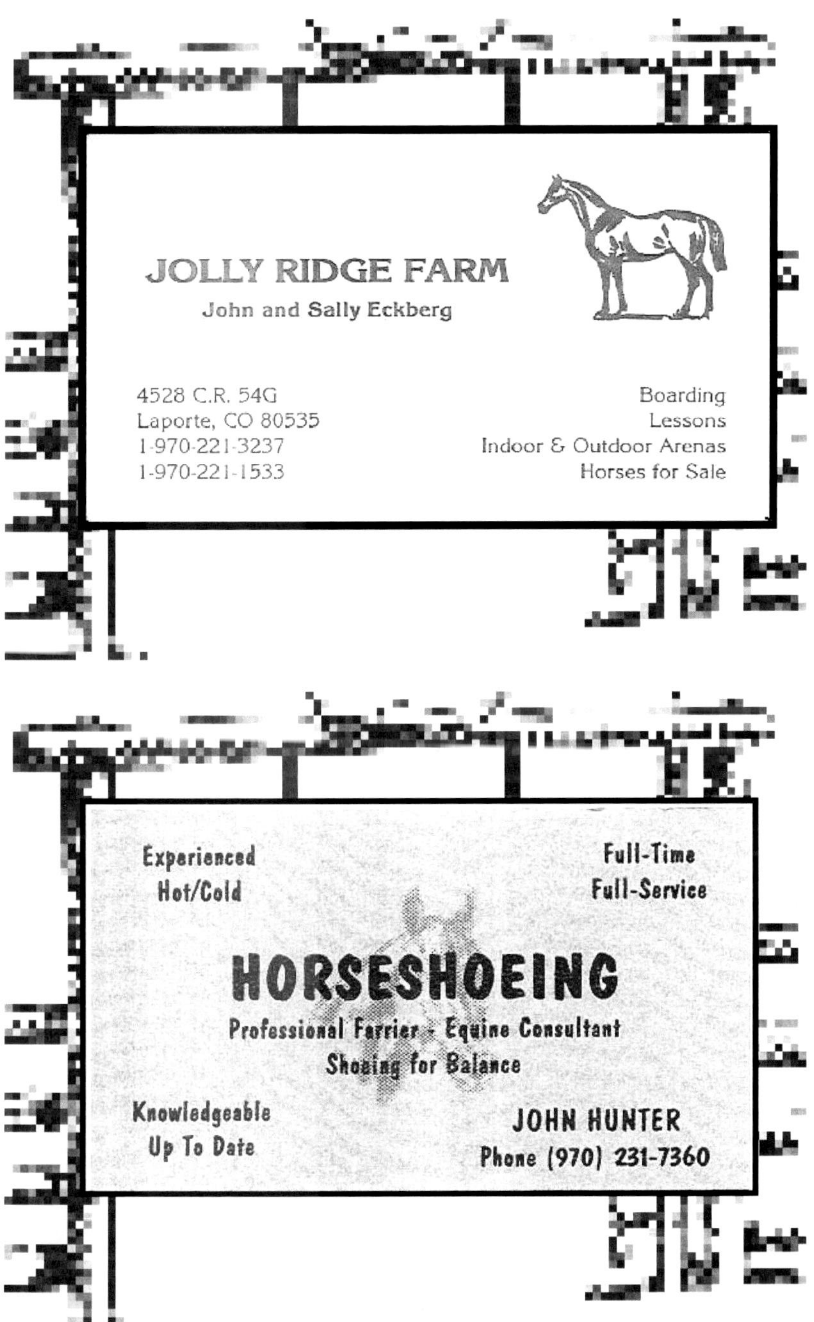

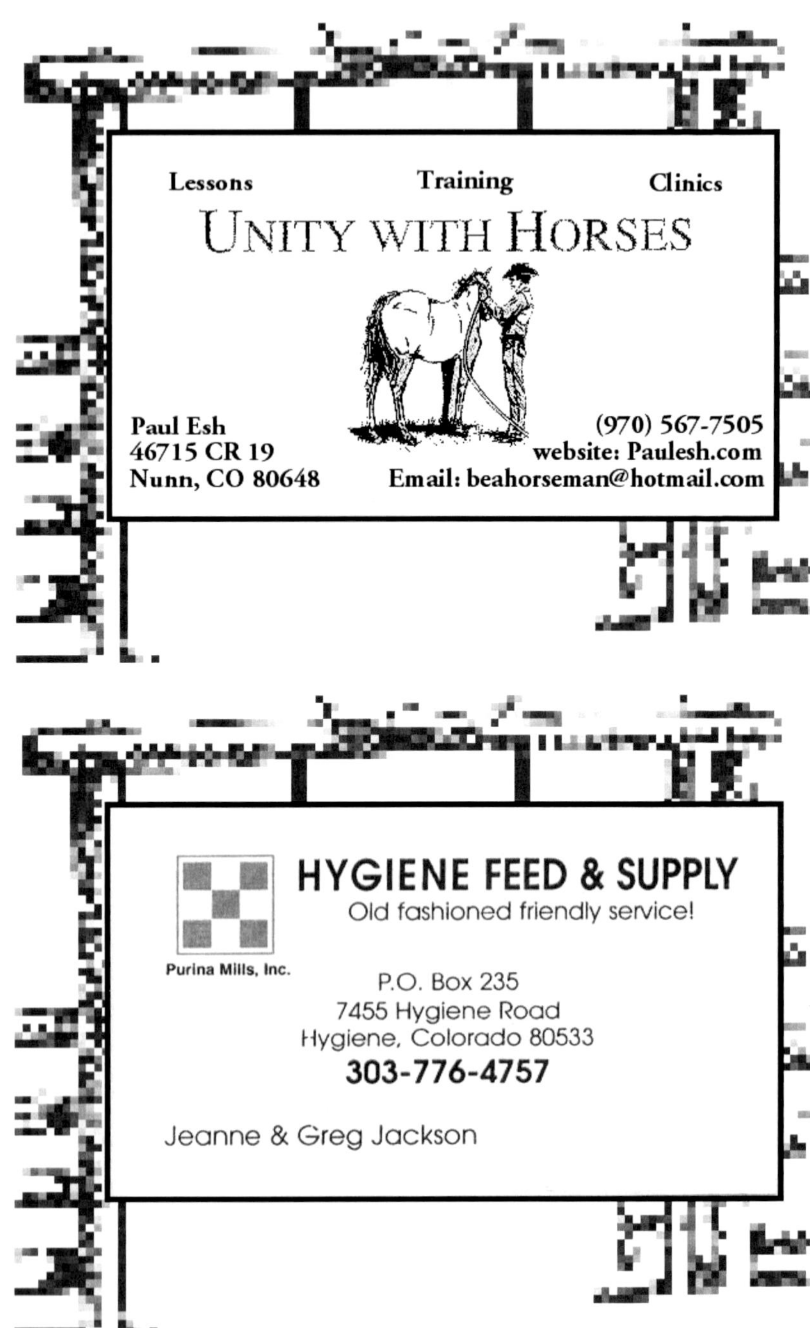
Lessons
Training
Clinics
UNITY WITH HORSES
Paul Esh
46715 CR 19
Nunn, CO 80648
(970) 567-7505
website: Paulesh.com
Email: beahorseman@hotmail.com
HYGIENE FEED & SUPPLY
Old fashioned friendly service!
Purina Mills, Inc.
P.O. Box 235
7455 Hygiene Road
Hygiene, Colorado 80533
303-776-4757
Jeanne & Greg Jackson

The Card Corral

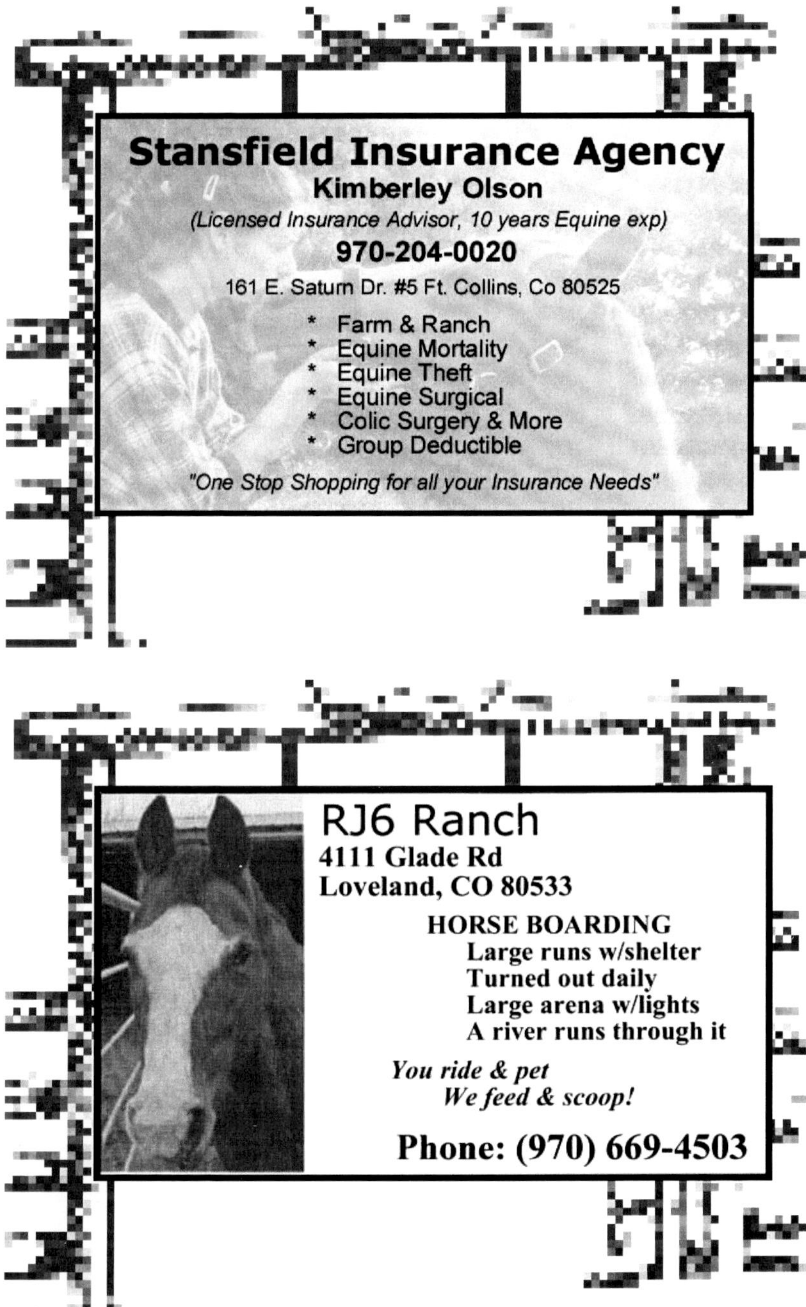

The Card Corral

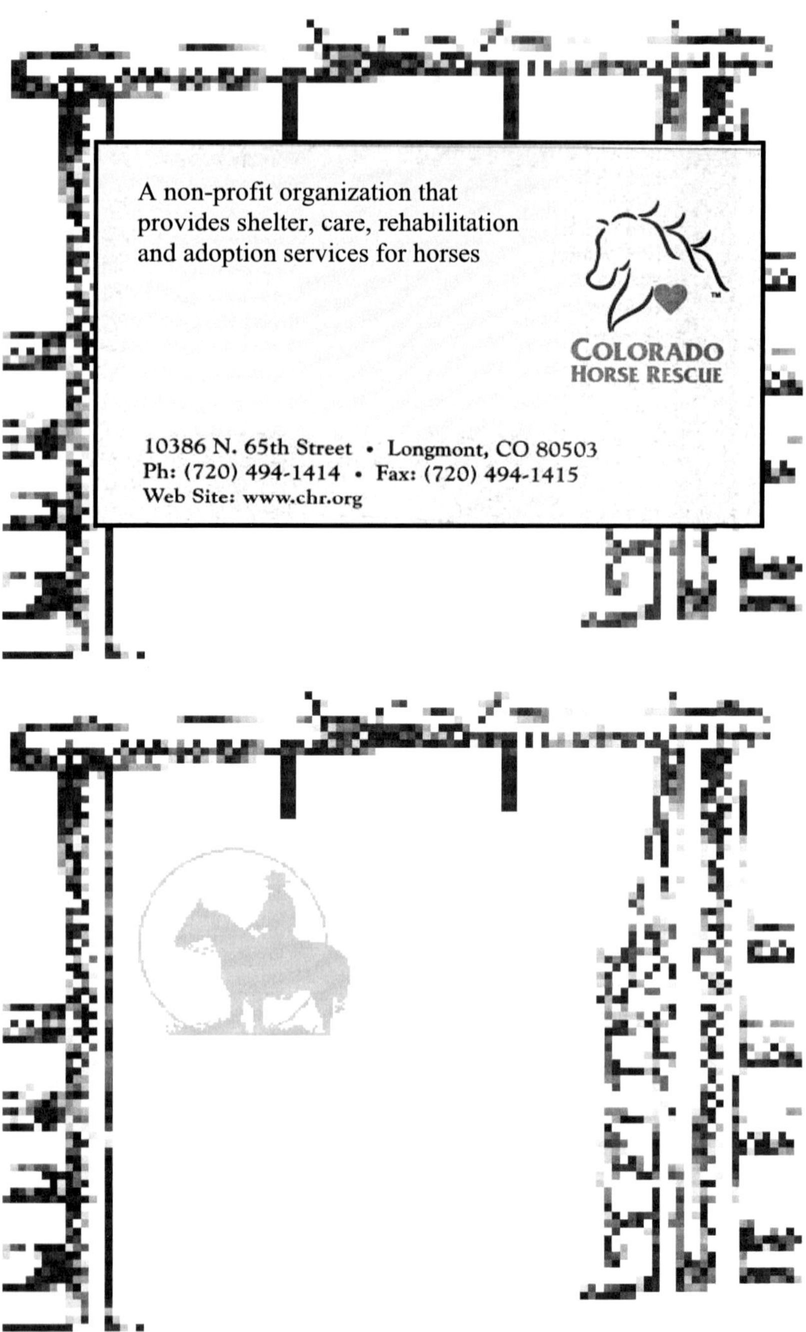